LIVING LIFE AS A WRITER

Ronna Fay Jevne, Ph.D.

Other books by Ronna Jevne

It all begins with hope: Patients, caregivers and
the bereaved speak out.

Voice of hope: Heard across the heart of life.

Hoping coping and moping: Handling life when
illness makes it tough.

Hope in practice: Selected conversations. (Editor)

Louis' Path.

Tea for the Inner Me: Blending tea with reflection.

Images and Echoes: Exploring your life with
photograpy and writing. (Editor)

Celebrating 60.

Zen and the Art of Illness.

No time for nonsense: Self help for the seriously
ill. With Alexander Levitan

Striving for health: Living with broken dreams.
With Harvey Zingle

When dreams don't work: Professional caregivers
and burnout. With Donna Williamson

The Hope Journal: With Jean Gurnett

Finding hope: Seeing the world in a brighter light.
With Jim Miller

Tellwell Talent
www.tellwell.ca

ISBN
978-0-2288-1275-3 (Hardcover)
978-0-2288-1273-9 (Paperback)
978-0-2288-1274-6 (eBook)

DEDICATED TO IRENE

Late on the evening of the death of my father, I sat in the moonlit living room of our country home, the fireplace lit, herbal tea in my hand. Allen had wisely retired, drained from the many demands of the day, knowing tomorrow would present no fewer. Across from me sat Irene with whom I have had the most enduring friendship of my life, now numbering more than 50 years, the entire duration without a harsh word ever exchanged.

My father once commented on the aging process, "It is one thing to make new friends, another to lose the ones that you made the memories with". Despite living apart much of our adult lives, it is with Irene that I made the memories, at least those memories that one makes outside of the inner sanctum of their own home. It is with Irene, on that painful day that another life was envisioned, a decision made, a commitment promised. I would begin my life as a writer. It was no surprise to either of us.

This one is for you Irene, for the words I haven't been able to say, not because of unwillingness but because of the limits of language to say "Thank you."

ENCOURAGEMENT TO WRITE

In this exquisite book, Ronna examines the essential questions, "What does it mean to be a writer? "What is it to live the life of a writer?"

Like a jeweller faceting a diamond, the many faces of challenge and possibility that writers face sparkle under her fierce gaze. There are sentences whose wisdom and beauty had me scrambling for a pen to write them in my own notebook. For example, she says, "I will write because writing has the potential to make a difference in someone's life, even if it turns out to only be in my own life." She convinces us that publication is lovely, but it's not the point. Writing is the point. She reminds us, "I need to welcome the words that come from that place of deep and quiet courage. The words that speak to what it means to become human, the words that open the heart to wrestle with the unspoken questions that we collude to avoid. I need to understand that I am a writer and this is my task."

As I read this book for review, over and over again, I was moved, by one chapter or another, to wish that I had a printed copies that I could offer to the participants in my workshops who are struggling with the very practical and philosophical issues she raises.

In this book, new and experienced writers alike, will be encouraged to write, finding inspiration and hope to craft words that pulse at the heart.

Sue Reynolds
Writer, Writing Facilitator, Psychotherapist
www.inkslingers.ca
www.goforwords.com

TABLE OF CONTENTS

Heeding the Call to Write

Dipping into the well

Responding to Distractions

Minding the Mundane

Listening for the Inspiration

Preparing to Write

Finding the Feeling

Walking the Write Path

PREFACE

My life as a writer began September 15, 2005. To the frequent question, "Why September 15?", I could reply only that September 1st was too soon, and October 1st was too late. Our lives needed editing to accommodate the shift. Without even a whisper of reservation, Allen embarked with me on the necessary steps to embrace a new identity, in some ways for both us. A quartet of support was complete with the full endorsement of Lynda and Sandi, chosen sisters, who, on the day of commencement delivered writing pads and sharpened pencils to my doorstep and insisted on not staying, on not interrupting my first day of life as a writer.

What will it be like to live my life as a writer? For more than thirty years, I have been a health care professional. My days have been filled with other peoples' problems. As a therapist and psychologist, a deep caring and curiosity for the complexities of the human phenomena were at the core of my work. As a professor, I loved the passion of students intent on making a difference in the lives of their clients. Throughout my career, I have been struck by our common humanity, by the misdemeanors of fate that separate the helpers from the wounded. The ethics of my work and the nature of my discipline have mandated that the stories to which I have been privy must remain silent. Those narratives remain in my heart as one of the sources of inspiration for my writing.

I have often felt like an introvert leading an extroverted life. What would it mean to be out of the public arena? Not speaking in public. Not chairing committees. Not having routine. Not going to the office. Not having a boss or colleagues or eager students. What would it be like to "be at home"- writing?

Some would say, indeed have said, "You are already a writer". Perhaps so, but I have not lived my life as a writer. Writing has been the backstage of my life. Late nights and occasional writing retreats have been productive but I have never had the privilege of having writing as the focus of my life. Although life as a writer may be a mythical state, I am interested in how life will be different, in how the writing process will be different - or similar.

How will I transition to this new identity? What will I notice? About myself? About the writing process? About how others view my choice? Will I develop a routine?

This collection of 300-400 word reflections began as *warm ups* to my writing time. Some are serious. Some are light. Some are driven by image. Some are complemented by image. Despite the temptation to generalize my experience to that of other writers, I have stayed with personal reflections while granting to all other writers the right to be as quirky as I sometimes am.

Beginning

Living Life
as
a Writer

Heeding the Call to Write

Saying *yes* to the call tends to place you on a path where half of yourself thinks that it doesn't make a bit of sense, but the other half knows your life won't make sense without it.

Gregg Levoy

Photo by S. Holzer

Entering life as a writer

I always knew that there would be another era to my life, a time when the obligations would recede and the call to the creative would draw me to the longed for solitude of the life of a writer. The moment of transition has come. With the dedication of the scribes of a cloistered monastery, my fingers slip across the keyboard in deliberately chosen stillness.

In anticipation, there were moments I had envisioned writing pages longhand while nestled into the old, yet classic slider rocker, the one piece of furniture that I know will be among the few artifacts of my life. The original outrageous purchase price has long since affirmed the adage, "You get what you pay for."

I have chosen to retain that wonderful rocking chair as a resting place, a place for tea and a good read. Learning to write in my office will best serve me in the long run. Where the natural light reveals the seasons. Where the reading chair is not far from the writing desk. Where Molly can lie at my feet, faithful companion for hours on end. Where the technology of writing and editing is present, yet not intrusive. Where I have the option of quill and ink, or pencil or keyboard. Where Annie Dillard's, *The Writing Life* and Brenda Ueland's, *If You Want to Write* are there to remind me that "It's okay to be a writer."

Perhaps it is even important to be a writer, not for the world, but for myself.

It is time to let my soul weave together the threads of my life that are becoming a tapestry of great satisfaction. It is hard to imagine exchanging any of the gifts experience has offered. No challenge seems wasted. No relationship is insignificant. No story is irrelevant. No age is preferred. No wound is meaningless.

It is time to listen to the call that invites me to the life of a writer.

Photo by G. Ross

Turning the corner ahead

If I am entering into life as a writer, am I leaving a life of something else? For days, that question has lingered. Am I coming from and therefore going to something? At a level of logic, I am leaving something and going to something new and different. At an existential level, it simply feels like I am turning a corner on the road in a direction that has always been intended.

It is time to leave the world of research proposals, competitive funding, center stage performances, and constant deadlines. It is time to shift from the outside world to the inner world. It is time to notice an inner life that has been unattended at times, given enough to more than survive, but not enough to flourish. It is time to recognize as did Ann Lindberg in the *Gift of the Sea,* "My life cannot implement in action the demands of all the people to whom my heart responds."

I am reminded of June Callwood who wrote in *Dropped Threads*, "I don't know what death is, but it can't be worse than the curse of an optimistic nature that learns nothing from discouragement" and only paragraphs later wrote, "The other truth I know concerns apathy, which I have on good authority (Hannah Arendt) is a workable definition of evil." It is in that vein that I share Caldwell's sense of life as a "predicament".

The passion for causes remains, but the energy for them is depleted. Retirement on the golf course or to a quilting group and a book club, is an option that I will not choose. The social democrat in me could not tolerate full time golfing, and the introvert that I am would go mad retiring to quilting and a book club.

When I review the sphere of influence of my professional activities, it is my writing that has touched people the most - the rural widow, the burned out nurse, and the breathless lung cancer patient.

I may write without the drive for publication. I will write because writing has the potential to make a difference in someone's life, even if it turns out to only be in my own life. Now I can write.

Making a difference

When I let myself drift into thinking that writing is not an activity worthy of a full commitment, I have to convince myself to keep writing. Others are out there doing significant things. Climbing Mt. Kilimanjaro to raise money for the Alzheimer's Society, assisting an Aids community in South Africa, training the psychologists of the future, researching deadly diseases, raising the food that sustains us, developing new ways of delivering distance learning, advocating for First Nations, and saving endangered species, to name only a few. Surely those are all more commendable than punching little keys and making letters appear on a screen. The comparison trap is there, no question.

Few of us are raised believing that writing is more than a hobby. If you don't golf in your spare time, perhaps you write, or quilt, or scrapbook.

Being blessed with the need for purpose is a potential curse that brings with it the tendency to rank the merit of purposes. Combine those tendencies with the value that society places on the need to produce income, and it becomes a recipe for doubt that writing is a justifiable pursuit. Having been part of making a difference in visible ways and knowing the satisfaction of doing so, there are tugs to return to 'real' work.

Those whose efforts directly address the disenfranchised are doing *hope work*. Living the life of a writer is also hope work. The hope for enjoyment, enrichment, knowledge, wisdom, justice, courage, and change is augmented by the written word.

Sometimes a few words can comfort or inspire, heal or help in ways that an author may never even know. One doesn't necessarily write to influence, but writing may influence. Minimally it invites integrity to my own life, calling me to honestly explore my own views, to dwell with ideas, to dance with creativity where possible. Still though, a little part of me craves the adventure of a rugged climb, the rush of a white water excursion, the fulfillment of helping a weary soul, the delight of holding the unjust accountable. Living my life as a writer neither excludes purpose nor adventure, but it does require that I co-exist with my reflections.

Accepting my limitations

It is ten at night. This is my first chance to sit in the quiet of a mountain cabin, television in the background, an empty popcorn bowl beside me, the man I love only an arm's length away. This particular day has brought me a deeper understanding of my strengths and a bolder realization that an ordinary day is an encounter with the gifts of many. Through the day, the skills of others enriched my life.

Today was the third treatment for a cervical injury incurred in a motor vehicle accident. With a high degree of expertise, a compassionate, quiet spoken, reassuring physician relieved pain that has defied all other approaches. This was something others, including myself, were not skilled to do. My physician is competent in ways that I am not.

Later, I arrived at the Canon Service Center where everyone in the office looked under thirty, seemed calm and exuded confidence as they moved about in a professional yet friendly ambience. A young technician saved my Canon D-10 SRL camera from major surgery with a simple fix. Two previous independent consultations had led me to accept serious and expensive repairs were in order, if not replacing the camera. People with technical callings seem to have a confidence that they will discover a solution. My camera guru is clearly competent in ways that I am not.

Still later in the day, I drove by a house my brother is constructing. He has the skill set required for the task, a skill set for which I don't even have the language to discuss. Clearly my brother, Nels, is competent in ways that I am not.

I am unable to relieve intractable pain, repair a camera sensor, or build a home. That's why we have physicians, digital consultants, and carpenters. The list of my inadequacies is limitless yet not limiting.

Within the world of writing, I have not decided if I will take on the tasks associated with publishing and marketing. Hopefully, the gods will just send me an agent/publisher/editor all in one affordable package. I am clear and confident that my task is to use my talents writing. Realizing my limitations and using others' competencies does two things. It accelerates the publishing process, and it creates free time to pursue my true passion of writing.

Writing as healing

Ask readers, "What helped you through your divorce, or through your grief, or what inspired you to go for your dream?" Commonly, they will tell you about something they have read. The self-help section of a bookstore is a well-browsed array of advice written by distant healers. Say to a writer, "You are a distance healer" and the response would likely be a puzzled frown.

What have you read that spoke to you at a deep level? It could as easily have been a poem as a novel, an essay, or a play. What touched you may have been in a book, in a magazine, or on a poster. It might have been fiction or non-fiction. Literature can touch our souls. As a young person, *Dr. Hudson's Secret Journal* was the impetus for me to start the life-long practice of journaling. I am sure that Lloyd Douglas had no idea that he would change my life.

I now understand the expression, "in the particular is the universal." I understand that as a reader you may resonate with my struggle or my strength; you may feel what I felt as you read what I have written. You may grow with me, as I grew through the events I describe. As an author, I am present through my words yet absent in your life.

Long before the formal profession of counseling or psychotherapy, there was literature. We learned who were the bad guys in life and who were the heroes and what it takes to make it in the world. We imagined, through the characters of the classics, the pain of loss, and the pride of achievement. Writers were teachers; writers were healers; writers were leaders. They taught and healed and led with the written word. They still do. Something I write may be healing to you. Something you write may be healing to me. Even a letter, a thank you note, a reference letter may make a difference in my life. We will likely never know when we are healing or helping in absentia.

Over the years, the symbolic nature of prayer flags has intrigued me. Where they are hoisted is blessed with the spirit of the person being honored. And so it is with words offered to the unknown reader.

Authoring our lives

For years, I have used writing as a therapeutic tool for myself having begun journaling at the age of 16 following the reading of *Dr. Hudson's Secret Journal.* For more than 30 years I have encouraged and facilitated clients and professionals to use written forms of disclosure and exploration to notice their feelings and their lives. Ira Progoff, a founding father of therapeutic writing and author of *At a Journal Workshop* believes that if you use the process he developed, you will never need a therapist. I am tempted to agree.

Many people begin journaling only to feel ineffective at any resolution of the issue they are addressing. Their stream of consciousness yields little insight and less action. Without additional writing tools, the exploration comes to a stand still. The value of journaling workshops is that they expand one's writing toolkit. For me, a writing toolkit is not complete without a camera.

A camera lets my eye tell me about my "I". The language of photography is the langauge of in-sight, focus, perspective, depth, framing, light, darkness. What is outside of my awareness often will apear in the image. When I put words to the images, I often understand what would have gone unnoticed if I had used only one medium. Aristlotle is credited with saying, "The soul never thinks without a picture." In his day, there wasn't the option of recording what the eye saw. Now we have both words and photographs to invite us to our inner work.

Lynn Nelson in *Writing and Being* says that we must publish our wounds and if we do not that our wounds will disclose themselves in our way of being and in our behavior. Each time I read her well-crafted words to clients, a silence follows as they recognize their need to disclose the gashes that have brought them to our conversation. Many are willing to explore the events and scars through writing, and now a burgeoning body of evidence supports the value of doing so.

Are those who use writing therapeutically really writers? Perhaps they are in that writing is allowing them to re-story their lives. Is there anything more important for us to author than our own lives?

Preferring book over article

When I was a professor, I was expected to publish as part of my work. No one ever asked me about writing. Now that I have chosen an identity as a writer and at least momentarily am unconcerned or at least not obsessing about publishing, I get asked questions I never before considered. The most recent was, "Why do you find a book easier to write than writing an article?" For me, there is no question that a book is easier. But why?

Academic articles have a protocol. They are fill-in-the-blanks kind of writing, a little like paint by numbers. The challenge is to focus on replying to a number of implied questions. The article must answer standard questions. What is the question or issue being addressed? Why is it important? What is the background to the concern including who has already said what about it? What is the author challenging or professing is new? What evidence is there for the argument, and what are the implications for practice? The audience for academic writing is small, a few authors and a few readers, many of whom are familiar with each other. We read each other's work to approve or disapprove, for membership in the club, for brownie points for our annual reports. Occasionally, a scientific book written in the vernacular will find its way to bookstore shelves.

A book is or can be a journey, a conversation with the author, a peek into their practice or a window into their life. I pack my bags and go with the author. The author shows me the landscape. We take side tours and adventures and once in a while we get lost. Good books don't crunch everything into a standard form like an application for a fast food chain position. I never feel part of an article, never feel necessary as a reader. With a book, I feel the author needs me, invites me to fill in the blanks, to create along with her. When I write, I am the host, ushering you into my universe, sharing my images and my adventures, even into my suffering. As a writer, I need my reader. We are in a close relationship with each other even though we will likely never meet. You read my words to join me in my world. I am writing my words to include you.

Finding my place on the landscape

How do I locate myself relative to other writers? Never having been a joiner, I suspect I will not be a member of a writing group, attend meetings of this or that guild, and despite the obvious alleged benefits will rarely find myself among a community of writers. I don't want to read drafts out loud to strangers and rarely wish to discuss with them what I am writing. Despite not being prone to guilt, I feel somewhat badly that I am not particularly interested in critiquing other authors or identifying myself with any sub-set of people whose preoccupation is with the written word. Yet, I do harbor a curiosity about writers whose writing evokes people to action, and to reflection. How did each of them live the life of a writer?

Presently at least, writer's block seldom paralyses me. As an introvert I have few cravings for companionship to interrupt the treasured solitude. I have acquired ample discipline. I am familiar with the steadfastness needed to write and the persistence needed to publish. Stepping away from leadership has offered a welcome reprieve from the need to be constantly politically correct- a potential barrier to honest writing. Having inhaled many books about writing, written by writers, I have concluded there is simply no recipe for success or satisfaction. Many authors have offered gold nuggets that I have clung to, and others I donated to the local garage sale.

Not withstanding numerous possible motivations, perhaps at my age it is sufficient to simply not want to join or participate in the common rituals of the profession. For me there may be an inherent danger in doing so. Doris Grunback in *Fifty Days of Solitude* most closely approximates my fear of impotence by exposure when she says, "Every ounce of acknowledgement of one's worth, however little, by the outside world, each endorsement of what I have become (no matter how insignificant), puts me in danger. In order to move forward in my work and deeper into the chambered nautilus of the mind that produces it, I need to retreat from praise..."

I need to write from a landscape of freedom, uncontaminated by need for approval.

Dipping into the well

What makes the desert beautiful is that somewhere it hides a well.

Antoine de Saint-Exupery

We never know the worth of water 'til the well is dry.

Thomas Fuller, Gnomologia, 1732

Drink water from your own cistern and from the springs of your own well.

Proverbs 5:15

Tasting a writer's life

The most productive writing experience I ever had was in a Swedish stuga. Because of travel complications and with the generosity of friends, I found myself in a 200-year-old Stuga awaiting the next leg of my vacation. These small cabins are sprinkled in the timberland of the countryside, just beyond the viable farmland. Like our "cabins at the lake" but for the most part much simpler, they serve as momentary getaways from the demands of the day. Initially disappointed at the interruption to my plans, I settled in with the only two English books *Veronica Decides to Die and The Da Vinci Code.* I supplemented them with two notebooks and an ever-sharp pencil that always accompanies me.

At the local grocery, I stocked up on herring, gluten free bread, cornmeal, soymilk, cans of chickpea, a few eggs, blueberry juice, a well-filled bag of Swedish soft candy, and tea. The blessing of having market gardeners as friends meant home grown loganberries, freshly grown potatoes, onions, fresh grapes reserved only for personal use from the vines of their greenhouse, and unlimited tomatoes and cucumbers. Fresh mushrooms were as close as the front door. I was assured that they were edible. The fireplace was supplemented with a hot plate.

There was ample natural light with windows on three sides and two small electrical lamps. Surely this was the recipe for a week of writing - one pot cooking, virtually no cleaning, rising with the sun and retiring with the sunset, no phones, faxes or fridge, and a week uninterrupted except for tea with Hans and Inga, the elderly couple down the lane. The intermissions with them were delightful as I struggled to bridge languages and cultures. Their unobtrusive yet watchful eye was like a warm comforter that wrapped me in a week of creative life.

The words poured out as the quiet poured in. The solitude, deepened by the gentle rain that pattered on the roof, was a long lost companion. This was a taste of a writer's life as I had never imagined. It was a coming home not knowing that I had been away. The writing flowed, day after day; the way a writer hopes it will and seldom does.

Photo by P. Jevne

Taking time to reflect

A reflective life takes time but so does repeating the stupid moments of our lives. New tears inform. Tears of repeated errors torment. If life is a series of teachable moments, I prefer new lessons.

When I am 80, I want to feel 80. I want to have earned the wrinkles, enjoyed the peace, known what my life was about. I want to be endeared to my errors and unrepentant for the adventures that went wrong. The stories I tell will have morsels of wisdom and an abundance of humor. The characters will be complex and their motives, on occasion, still puzzling. Those who read my memoirs will be perplexed at how little of me they knew, and I will delight in them being mystified.

What I will have held back will not be a function of shyness, or embarrassment or any sense of apology for my actions, but a deep sense of not wanting to be a wholly public, transparent person.

I want to have enjoyed noticing my life. Not wake up at some undesignated age wondering where I have been and what I have been doing for 20 years, unable or unwilling to accept responsibility for what were essentially my choices.

The process of reflection is a way of calling myself home, to what I value, to what makes sense to me, to what hurts and what delights me. Without awareness, I have no choices. Without choices, I have no life. Even when the choices are seemingly limited, I have the choice of an inner life that finds a rightful place for what I experience as unjust or difficult.

Awareness rarely happens without reflection, and solitude is the place where reflection begins.

Living the life of a writer positions me to become reflective. It is no guarantee of wisdom though. When I refuse to enter into solitude, I am refusing to enter life as a writer as I envision it.

Writing is ultimately an alone endeavor.

Going inside

To live the life of a writer means going inside, exploring what is seemingly not visible. Or is it? Many writers are entertainers, have no particular need for reflection, and indeed even avoid the darkness of the human soul. There are genres which feel so foreign to me I have no doubt they exceed my skill. I simply cannot envision that I would be interested or capable of writing with the complexity needed for some mystery or adventure plots. Since I don't read them, it is unlikely I would write them. Whether I don't read them for the same reason I wouldn't write them, I am not sure.

When it comes to fiction, I like few characters and a limited setting. Sometimes I reread the stories in *Photocopies* by John Berger to remind myself of the power of fewer words, rather than many. I yearn to write with the focused precision that Sandor Marai achieves in *Embers*. As for description, I want the author to leave something for my imagination to fill in. I don't want to read detail that is essentially minutia. As a reader, my interest wanes if there is nothing for me to do but consume. Might as well see the movie. Humor will never be a genre for me although I am appreciative of those skilled at it. Robert Fulgrum is a master at making the everyday entertaining. Others who try for full out funny simply don't make it with my psyche.

Writers like Michael Ignatieff amaze me. How does an author develop the capability to write equally powerfully a treatise on ethics and an engaging novel? Living the life of a writer will include reading others' works, noticing what it is that they attend to, noticing what I am drawn to, experimenting with unfamiliar genres, claiming and reclaiming my own voice.

This is not a wholly new life. My professional experience as a scholar and therapist and my personal experience as a journal writer are like pillars that will join with my reflective and creative nature to launch the life of a writer. I need to remember I am going inside to complement my being, not exchanging my whole life.

Being an active voyeur

How do I deal with my ambivalence about being a voyeur of life in my own community, more interested in describing the dynamics of what is happening than influencing them? Small town politics are very serious. Sitting at the shit disturbers' table at the local pot luck legion supper is a political statement and more fun than occupying a chair at a neutral table.

Attending church services in a 105-year-old rural church is more an act of community than an act of worship. Its members number fewer than 30, depleted, not by the rural to city drift but by the attraction to churches with a calendar of organized activities, multiple pastors, a real budget, the sense of belonging to something successful, and the anonymity of not being noticed if attendance lapses.

Somehow though, in church the annual pie sale doesn't carry with it the same personal touch of knowing that a handful of moms spent all day Saturday mentoring local teenagers in the art of pie making.

The local museum represents thousands of hours of work of dedicated volunteers, mostly seniors. Their will to preserve the hundred years of local history is relentless. Bake sales, raffles, small grants, and estate legacies advance the cause. The pride of local families and the courage of the pioneer spirit are palpable among the war memorials, the historical dentistry exhibit, and the Women of Aspen biographies.

The local eateries are not exactly cosmopolitan. If I want Indian, Japanese, Ukrainian or Scandinavian food, I will need to drive an extra 40 kilometers. This is the same distance I travel to purchase vegan bouillon cubes, fresh tofu, gluten free imitation Oreo cookies, soy yogurt, or wild salmon.

The vendors of the local farmer's market offer fresh baking, some gluten free, free range eggs, home made sausage, fresh dried spices, fruit and relish preserves, and hand knitted baby blankets. These craftsmen, market gardeners, farmers, quilters and kitchen-based bakers are local culture.

Will I someday blend the characters and culture of my own community more into the prose that I write? How do I do so and yet respect the private lives of those I encounter? What ethical responsibility do I have as an author?

Seeing life as data

As a writer, all of life is data. No wonder I find photography and writing blending in my psyche. Writing, like photography, is about seeing. About seeing things from different perspectives, through different lenses. About noticing that image alone is not truth. That there may not be a single 'truth'. There may be a kaleidoscope of understandings.

My interpretations are subject to error - for as a writer, as a photographer, I am always outside of the experience I am recording. Nevertheless I must look, must search for a reasoned story. As a writer, I am committed to deepening and discerning the human experience, to making visible an inner life we each have, often outside of our awareness. The photographer in me is willing to let the image speak, to let the observer sift through his or her life for a likeness that evokes a response.

The writer in me torments myself with what went before and what will come after the embrace. Wonders if there are words exchanged in the embrace in this picture? She wonders if the story begins with "He was so proud" or "She was so sad", knowing either is possible. The photographer captures the moment, the writer hungers for the continuity of the moments that are the story.

How then, do I know to which images to attend, which stories to tell? As a photographer, when do I point the lens towards the ugly and when towards the gentle? As a writer, when do I write what Deena Metzger in *Writing for your Life* calls "the cover story" and when do I write the authentic, more painful story? I make many simple choices every day about how I spend my dollars, how I nourish my body, and how I use my time. Should I be any less concerned about how I dispense my thoughts, how I nourish my soul, what I offer to the village that is my world?

How able am I to live my remaining years as a writer true to the most treasured words of my mother's wisdom, "Never for the sake of civility or social graces forego your own truth?"

Gathering memories

Blustery days have been announcing the coming of fall. Going outside requires a heavy sweater and a windbreaker now. There is a nip in the air that only October brings. Yesterday even a brief walk was a forced choice. Accompanied by my camera, in simple dedication to an often neglected body, I explored the paths of the Rundle Mission Heritage site. The crunch of the leaves was hardly audible over the rustle of the gentle breeze generated through the aspen grove. It seemed a perfect day to come across an old country graveside. The sole occupants are Simon Fraser and his wife buried there in 1922 and 1918 respectively. A quiet settled over me as I wondered how they might have come to rest in this unassuming plot.

Today is summer's last cough. Today the autumn stillness is as remarkable as yesterday's winds that stole the illusion of Indian summer. In place of an overcast sky, there is a prairie blue one with white puffs like only an amateur artist would paint. Not a leaf moves. The lake reflects a near mirror image of its shores. Yesterday, even a brief kayak paddle would have been demanding. Days like today are surely numbered. Within weeks the snow flurries will bring us our next season. The kayaks will be bedded for the winter, geese will be absent from the skies, and the waiting will again begin.

Today when I walk, my camera will once again be on my shoulder, ready to capture images of the transitions to another season. This is a day to leave the keyboard, to don my walking shoes and to join my camera in seeing my world. It is time to let the warmth of the sun say good-bye to summer and to let the sound of the silence enter into my soul. As a squirrel gathers nuts for the winter, it is time to gather memories for writing.

Writing for ten minutes

One of the myths I tell myself is that I need "uninterrupted time" to write. I rarely say how much uninterrupted time I need. I used to hold up in the Sylvia Hotel in Vancouver for a week to concentrate on a manuscript. And it worked. I just didn't have enough weeks at the Sylvia. Once every couple of years was a treat. Escaping from the responsibilities and routine of a 24/7 life into a week dedicated to writing was like a fish going from a polluted aquarium to the freedom of an ocean. It didn't hurt to be able to see the actual ocean out the oak framed window of the old part of the hotel.

One year a friendly mouse, escaping from the cold coastal spring, with my blessing shared the room. We were good roommates. He never approached the desk. I never chased him away from the heat register. I refused to have a trap set or to allow the hotel cat to join me. Both seemed too violent. I just wanted to write. He just wanted to be warm. That seemed fair.

If I don't have a week, I know a ten-minute write will suffice. The power of a ten-minute write came home to me while attending a Zen Writing Practice Retreat[1]. Over and over the power of story written in ten minutes and only ten minutes flowed out. The pain of a neglected child, the grief of a widowed lawyer, the joy of a loved parent, the triumph of a mountain climbed, the pride of a garden planted. Fiction or fact. No one will ever know. No one ever has to. The ten minute write leaves no time for reflection, no time to hum and ha about this word or that. No time to shuffle papers or to worry about accuracy that can be researched later. Just write. Write.

Keep the pen moving. Keep the pen moving. Whole books could be written with ten-minute writes. I still take solace in the myth that I need uninterrupted time. It leaves me with at least one option for explaining failure or procrastination.

---

[1] For more information about Zen Writing Practice workshops see: www.zenwords.net

Visiting the library

I am visiting a library that has 2,000,000 volumes including only one of mine. I am ambivalent as I stand among the stacks both respecting and resenting that what I produce is and will always be but a drop in the ocean of recorded thought. Among the tomes are many that have never been selected by a reader. They lie in wait, not yet cherished by the unknown reader. I still love the silence of a library. I love walking down the aisles trying to make sense of the coding system, feeling accomplished when I secure the one among thousands for which I was looking.

When I browse in my favorite bookstore where the clerks are over 30 and they all actually read, I notice different things than in the culture of a library. In the world of commerce, the book jacket is all-important. In a library, only the spine is visible. Only the title draws the eye. In a library there are no bargain counters implying a book has been devalued. There are no posters for sale or picture frames on display. There is no General Sales Tax added to the cost of reading. Despite not having a coffee bar, my bookstore is somehow personal. It is MY bookstore. I know where to look for what I like to read yet small enough I can browse outside of my interest area. When there are no new books in the writing section, I am always pleased for reasons I have yet to understand. The photography and self-help section get just a walk-through as the former is most often too expensive, and the latter just annoys me despite once having been a regular visitor of that genre.

There are some books to which I return over and over, like *The Twelve Gifts of Birth* by Charlene Costanzo, which I give to the parents of every new child in my world, even if there isn't a baby shower.

A recent favorite is *Listening Below the Noise* by Anne D. LeClaire. *The Gift of the Sea* by Anne Morrow Lindbergh should bless the shelf of every woman over forty. As a writer, I hope that I might leave such a legacy. Might write such a classic. Might develop such a gentle honest form. It is about more than defying the adage that books "have the shelf life of lettuce". It is the effort towards timeless meaning that matters.

Browsing a book store

Calling myself a writer has changed the experience of browsing a bookstore. As I move from shelf to shelf, I now notice book jackets, titles, page and font sizes. I notice where my eyes go and what holds my attention. Understanding marketing is not the motivation. It is a searching for something I would call the 'integrity' of the book. There is no other word to which I am drawn.

When the cover illustration somehow matches the title, and both are congruent with the jacket blurbs, and the print is 'right' for the genre, my eyes linger longer - at least until I notice the price tag which these days is reliably hefty. The choice to purchase must represent what I value. Not too dry, not so conversational that a new age spiritual growth tape would have less filler, not cute or shallow, not the third version of the same material by the same author. As a reader, the critic in me is alive and well. Small bookstores, like Café Books in Canmore and Greenwoods in Edmonton had the same quality as the books I seek, that congruence that only intuition detects. There is little sense of them being prostitutes to promotional pressure, or that a publisher bought their eye level shelves. And there is rarely more than one or two copies of each treasure on display. Now Greenwoods has closed.

I am left to browse in the commercial culture of the popular bookstore and the coffee shop. Browsing is something a writer does, not something I am doing that is "wasting time" or something I am stealing time to do. By browsing, ideas seep in. There is inspiration by osmosis. Today, by browsing and actually purchasing *Making Journals by Hand* by Jason Thompson, the idea of doing a journal of the many notes Dad left, not full out reflections, just notes, tons of notes, was born.

How sorry I am for discarding the many cards and funeral memorials he kept. Nothing more will go until I have done *Field Notes of a Farmer.* How I wish Mom had left a similar soul trail to Dad's.

Bringing Zen to my practice

If you had said there would be a time when I would sit, often uncomfortably on my knees for thirty minutes, walk aimlessly for another twenty, write non-stop without concern for content or grammar for three consecutive 10 minute sprints, read to strangers without feedback, and then move an enormous rock or do some other mundane task all while keeping 'noble' silence, I would have said, "Sure, right after I vote for a conservative corporate candidate in a federal election! It will not happen."

Now I am happy to sit uncomfortably on my knees for thirty minutes, walk aimlessly for another twenty, write non-stop without concern for content or grammar for three consecutive 10 minute writes, read to strangers without feedback and then move a rock or do some other mundane task all while keeping *noble* silence.

I need to be free to write but tethered to a practice that enourages it. I am now deeply moved by a writing practice steeped in the ritual and respect of the Zen tradition. At a retreat, I am honored to repeat the pattern four or five times a day beginning at 6:00 am and ending at 10:00 pm, interspersed with simple food. I am not sure why. I simultaneously desire and dread each experience.

I have learned that during the process the monkey mind of my inner life swings from thought to thought until it begins to quiet in the silence. The silence is individual yet we are in community. The zendo, the makeshift temple, becomes our refuge. We enter and leave with a bow. We bow to our own sitting place and to those we sit with. The silence gives us permission to discard the routine niceties and to withdraw from the compulsion to explain – anything. What happens is not easily captured with words, but our words change us as we write. The words spew from our guts or bubble up from our hearts. Our heads cease to be the source of our writing, at least not the sole source. Nothing is censored. It just happens.

With a history of well-chosen words, well structured logic, and targeted audiences, it took months to let the control seep away through a sieve of *neither thinking, nor not thinking*. Initially the instruction was meaningless. It is now the writing space I most treasure.

Responding to Distractions

I like long walks, especially when they are taken by people who annoy me.

Noël Coward

Rejecting the muse

The saboteur lurks in the crevices of the frenetic pace of the unexamined life. A litany of small diversions is no less lethal than a major intrusion and less defensible.

Pack for the weekend
Plan for the guests
Write that letter
Call that friend
Shorten those slacks
Organize that drawer
Make that appointment

Bake that cake
Send that special card
Order that gift
Review that book
Write that grant proposal

Trade the car
Wash the rug
Groom the dog
Fix the washer
Sew on the button
Photograph the ball game
Submit the manuscript
Attend that funeral
Write my member of parliament
Prepare the low cal cheesecake
Re-do the guest room
Buy the hearing aid batteries
Order the poetry book

And on and on it goes.

Little wonder
Some days the muse
Does not re-visit.

Weaving in the interruptions

My mom was a remarkable woman. As a full time human resources consultant, she commuted an hour and fifteen minutes each way to work. Yet, as a farm wife, she never renounced the obligation of her role in making planting season and harvest go smoothly. Field lunches, unexpected trips to town for machinery repairs and first aid for the inevitable minor injuries of farm life, coupled with tending the typical sizable rural garden, canning, and grandchild care, often diverted her from the focus of her own passions. I recall her saying, "The interruptions to my work used to annoy me until I came to understand that the interruptions are my work." For her work, she was awarded a place in the Alberta Agricultural Hall of Fame; for her interruptions she was loved deeply by family and community.

There are times when the wisdom of her words revisit me. Wrapping Christmas parcels for overseas mailing, meeting with the accountant about my father's estate, taking time to make what is likely a last visit to a pioneer woman raised sister to my grandmother, encouraging a young academic overwhelmed with the challenges of her new position, promising tea and sanity to a young mother, agreeing to bring dessert to a pot luck - these are my work as well. This is my work as a person. This is the work that reminds me that I have a place in the hearts and lives of others. It is from that well that the spirit of writing flows.

There are other peripheral distractions, easily defined as interruptions but actually directly related to living my life as a writer. Writing proposals, doing research, editing, contacting co-authors, exploring funding sources, considering publishers, browsing bookstores for related writings, and acquiring computer skills to name a few.

These are part of the work of a writer. Resenting life, as if I could write well without it, or being annoyed at the less satisfying aspects of a writer's life would be to adhere to some free floating mythology about what it is to live the life of a writer.

It is just that some days, I wonder how mom did it. How did she so seamlessly weave the interruptions in to her life? I wonder how I will weave together the parts of my life into a satisying tapestry.

Walking away is okay

There is no place in the house where I can't hear the television. Where the commercials can't reach me. Where the distraction doesn't irk me. No amount of concentration blocks out stimulation. No sentence flows easily with the incessant invasion of noise in the background. It is impossible for me to create characters while other characters I didn't create are racing cars, shooting guns, barking rude remarks or being dramatic about everyday life.

Most television rots the soul. Special effects and blaring backgrounds substitute for real life. Television offers a world of encounters I don't identify with. I am not an unhappy housewife, a wanna' be singer, chef or designer. I don't enjoy crude humor and am even tiring of the late night news that informs me I live in a threatening world. Recently, I decided I didn't want to watch more than one murder a day. Being married to a former police officer increases the probability that I will watch crime shows.

Even when, or perhaps particularly when, I view television from the perspective of a writer, I wonder, "Who is the audience? Who watches this trivia?". Yet, I feed at the feast of intellectual junk food far too often. A good movie or an informative documentary seems different. I am offered something to think about, something to reflect upon.

Is the world of the written word any different? Are there not books for every taste? Is there not the inane and the inspirational, the factual and the fictional, the reflective and the superficial, the entertaining and the informative, the boring and the stimulating? Clearly there are only a few topics, a few genres that I consistently enjoy. I don't read the ones I anticipate not enjoying. Yet, I watch television that doesn't nourish me. Indeed, it distracts me from writing, numbs my brain, and drains my creative inclinations. When? When? When will I learn to simply turn it off and read or write? Or leave the room when family is enjoying something I do not? I need to learn that it is okay to just walk away, to just head off in my own direction.

Tacking back to the task

Most women are multi taskers. It seems simple enough to throw the laundry in the washer while the sweet potato and millet cook for lunch. It's routine to answer phone calls while putting away the groceries. I crochet while I watch television. In the darkroom, I used to do deep knee bends while I waited for the developer chemicals to perform their magic. I can plan a supper for 30 in the time it takes to fold the laundry. I used to prepare and commit to memory my public lectures while I commuted.

There are activities and times that are not conducive to multi tasking. Answering an overabundance of e-mails seems to be a solo task. Thank goodness for a very adequate spam detector that ended the penis extension offers! I have the capacity to use a laptop computer as a passenger in a vehicle but mostly I resist doing so. Somehow, traveling at a hundred kilometers an hour on a freeway or being surrounded by city traffic doesn't enhance creativity.

As a professor, a typical day included working on a research grant, teaching advanced counseling or research theory, meeting with confused or passionate students, supervising students in the clinic, reviewing a manuscript for a journal, and preparing an ethics clearance. In other words, multi tasking became multi-project-ing. Keeping a dozen balls in the air at once was the extension of multi-tasking.

Normally multi tasking seems to be a strength, yet it can be a problem for me. It disrupts my train of thought when I leave my office to stir the chili. My concentration is broken when I hear the dryer go off. When I "split screen", I am not fully engaged in the writing process.

All of me is not engaged in the activity of creating. This in itself is annoying. There is a second consequence, a subtle saboteur. I tend to have multiple projects on the go. In and of itself that might be fine. However, when the ratio is more starts than finishes, at some point a little work on each completes nothing. Chronic incompleteness is not encouraging to the writer within.

In the life of a writer, the challenge is to stay focussed, and like sailors, to tack back towards my destination, when the winds of life have blown me off course. With practice, I get back on course with less energy and in less time.

Decluttering the zone

It is the fall of my life. Time for clarity, not clutter. Yet, each morning despite what sometimes feels like Herculean efforts, there is clutter in my life. Some are mandated distractions. Some are needless diversions. All are countless invitations that tempt me to lose sight of the path I have chosen, constantly nudging me to put writing second.

Admittedly, the dog does need feeding, the plants need watering, the laundry must be done, the dishwasher must be emptied, the groceries must be put away, the car must be serviced, the bills must be paid, and occasionally, I must appear at social functions. I feel compelled to send birthday cards, to attend church occasionally, and to periodically write my elected representative in defense of Medicare.

Thank goodness any inclination to volunteer has passed, despite the admirable mission of the many well-intended causes.

The seasons themselves bring a form of clutter. On an acreage, spring requires planting, the summer requires tending, autumn requires harvesting, and winter requires stowing the yield necessary to tide one over for the next cycle. Indeed, some of what feels like the clutter of life is the manna that nourishes civilized living.

Less clutter means more time for writing. How and when I perform the mostly necessary trivia of life, reflects my loyalty to the call to which I say I am responding. By being undisciplined I, of course, run the risk of failure. However, I acknowledge there is a scarier scenario. By being disciplined, I also run the risk of failure. In the first instance, I am able to claim that had the world been gentler with me I might well have written an award-winning novel. In the latter case, I have to face the possibility that my talents are limited. In the real world, I must balance passion with practicality. Recently, a major edit of our home elevated the sense of order in our lives. Errands outside of our home have been allotted to Thursdays, the dog is now on a self-feeder, and our meals are simpler. Each morning, I rise with a childlike joy, long since subdued until recently, and I greet the day with, "Today I have the privilege of writing!"

Es-spousing the solitude

"You going to write this morning darling?"

"Yes"

"Great. I know you are really into that next chapter. I'll be in my workshop fixing the weed wacker. It is really giving me problems every time I try to start it."

"Okay, hon, thanks. Hope it goes well."

One hour in –

"Just wondering if you want a cup of tea, sweet heart?"

"Thanks hon, but I am on a roll here."

"Okay, you sure?"

"Yes, sweetie. I am sure."

Quiet pause, him still standing at the door,

"I couldn't fix the weed eater."

"You can usually fix anything."

"Well in a way I did fix it. I took the chop-saw and chopped the damn thing into little pieces."

"Seriously?"

"Yes, seriously. And I really enjoyed doing it. That damn thing hasn't worked for a year."

Me, not turning away from the computer,

"Okay. Glad you got it working, hon."

"You sure you don't want tea?"

"I'm sure."

Two hours in -

"I better go get another weed eater. Anything you need at the hardware store?"

"No, not that I can think of, thanks."

"Okay. I will be back in an hour."

Three hours in –

"I got the new weed wacker. How's the writing?"

"It's coming."

"What you planning for supper? Can I help?"

Silently I think to myself,

"Do we need to do everything together honey?"

Inspiration needs dedicated focus for expression. We are fortunate if we have supportive spouses who understand that writing is actual work. It is not just a hobby that fills in time between super-mom activities and taking mother-in-law to her medical appointment, and volunteering for the anti-freeway community lobby. Finding the balance between expressing appreciation and asserting some degree of boundaries to our emotional and physical writing space is an art. It requires gentle strokes on the canvas of our marriages.

Finding a rhythm

I learned to swim late in life. So pleased was I with mastering this long forbidden activity, now possible because of ear surgery, that I plunged in with fervor. Being naturally athletic, I quickly acquired the rhythm necessary for the basic crawl and within days prided myself on twenty consecutive laps. The next morning my head refused to turn either direction. Asked what I had been doing, I proudly confessed my achievement to my physician of twenty years. He replied, "Is that the way you do everything?" I confessed, "I suppose it is." He graciously refrained from further comment.

Not long ago, determined to find the gold nuggets in a highly recommended book, I persisted through 218 boring pages before abandoning the task. By then, I admitted that either "I simply didn't get it" or that I got the redundant message in the first chapter.

Meanwhile, my creativity was draining from me like an intravenous running in the wrong direction.

In a similar vein, mostly because of circumstance, we recently overdosed on guests. I normally love company and know one day it will not happen with today's regularity. Instead of the usual satisfaction of hosting people, there was a sense of being a food machine pumping out pleasant but soulless cuisine. My contributions to the conversation were not much better.

In like manner, just days ago I was so engrossed in a writing project that supper was late, and I was exhausted. The impromptu bland vegetarian meal that followed matched my vegetative state of mind! Writing was of no interest to me the following day.

When I overextend, within or outside of my awareness, my mind goes soggy and a soggy mind doesn't write. It doesn't even want to write. If I am to have non-writing days, I want them to be by choice, not a function of needless exhaustion. I wonder how long it takes for the rhythms to develop, to know how long and how hard to work at writing. How to pace and play in this new endeavor. In the intervening interval, as I craft a way of being while living life as a writer, I will remind myself to go gently.

Co-authoring is hard work

Teaming up with a co-author can be a blessing or a menacing distraction.

Co-authors from hell have little experience, often admit exactly that and yet refuse to make use of those with greater experience. They live in their heads despite wanting to write from their hearts. They insist on compound complex sentences, sophisticated punctuation, and an abundance of big words to tell even the simplest of stories. They want feedback but resist editing and confuse effort with fluency. They want the world to read their work, yet keep the readability index at 3rd year college!

Many books describe the pros and cons of co-authoring but no one says, "Here is how you make the decision to go it alone or co-author." Co-authoring is not the issue; co-authors are the issue. The question needs to be more specific.

"Co-author" with whom? About what?"

Some marriages work. Some just don't. When it comes to co-authoring, I have had both. Writing is hard enough. Hassling with a co-author makes it harder. There are people I know I can work with, people who I think I can work with, and people to whom I should outright say, "We are not a good match." Flattery was the trap I fell into a couple of times. Hard earned lesson #1, "Don't co-author because someone presents a convincing argument for being helpful." The manuscript will not likely see the light of day. Tutor but don't co-author.

I think I will do the rest of my writing life as a solo author. And yet, I know I won't. I have had too many good experiences. I enjoy the dialogue. I appreciate the enthusiast. I like the deadlines that inevitably move the project along more quickly. I love seeing the document fine tuned. Equally so, I am disturbed when I feel the passion being diluted by irreconcilable differences however masked with rationale and or politeness. Choosing a middle of the road alternative rarely makes for a good text.

There is a chemistry to co-authorship just like a good marriage. Both people have to work at it, and the energy has to be there from the beginning. Lesson #2, as Barbara Turner Vessalago would say: "Go where the energy is. If it isn't there, don't go there and don't stay there."

Minding the Mundane

A miracle every day would cease to be miraculous—it would be mundane. Though even a boring sunset is still glorious.

Jarod Kintz

Feasting on reading

There is a marked increase in my reading. Not an intended pursuit, just an offshoot I suspect of the focus on writing. In this first month, my selections have included *Embers* by Sandor Marai, a riveting account of two elderly men coming together to open or heal a 42 year old wound; *For Joshua*, by Richard Wagamese, a First Nations man and author reaching out to his estranged son in the medium that is his work; *On Becoming an Artist* by Ellen Langer, a conversational comment on 'how to' get on with being an artist; *Affluenza*, by Graff, Wann and Naylor, a social comment on the epidemic of consumption; *Survival or Prophecy: The letters of Thomas Merton and Jean Lecerq*, edited by P. Hart, a small window into the complex spirituality of two well known and respected monks; *Sea Kayaking*, by Shelley Johnson, basically instructional in nature; *Carry Me Across the*

Water by Ethan Canin, the reflections of a wealthy, yet humble once Jewish man who faces aging with humor and clarity; and *Thank You for Not Reading,* by Dubravka Uguresic, a commentary on the world of writing and publishing presented with astuteness and story. On my bedside remain *Wisdom,* by Robert Sternberg, *The History of God* by Karen Armstron, *At Seventy* by May Sarton and *Digging Deep* by Fran Sorin.

Let's see, that means novels, autobiography, 'how to', philosophy/religion, psychology, and gardening have all caught my attention. Two or three others whose titles I don't even recall were read and immediately put on the 'donate to a library' shelf. For one reason or another, they are not keepers. What does this mean for my writing? I have no idea.

What I do know is that I am once again reading for the sake of reading. The television is staying off. I actually sit in the high back office chairs I purchased for the purpose of reading. Surprisingly I eat less! What the relationship is to between reading more and eating less also escapes me, but I like it. Conversations with Allen have increased in frequency and depth, and we have inane discussions about the differences amongst journalists, historians and writers.

If I was never to pick up a pen or put my hands to the keyboard, the decision to live life as a writer has already had generous benefits.

Pleasing the palate

Maybe there is some truth to the metaphor of giving birth to a piece of writing. I am not consuming ice cream and pickles, but I do consume an unlikely assortment of victuals in the name of creativity. Normally, I snack out of boredom. In the context of writing, the low fat popcorn, miniature marshmallows, sweet pickles, cashews, and medjool dates act as some kind of alien fuel. Each stroll away from the keyboard is for a handful of something, and always only one thing. The munching protocol is like serial pilgrimages to the pantry, the fridge, or the microwave. I wish I could say, the fruit bowl.

The excursion is for a nibble, not a meal. Occasionally, I think of it as grazing. However, I never graze on carrot sticks, apples wedges, or left-over chili. There seems to be a direct inverse correlation to the frequency of the gastronomic distractions, if that is what they are, and the ease with which I am writing.

It makes little sense that three sweet pickles are required to access the right verb or the next phrase. Yet, as often as not, when I return to my workstation, the words flow again, if only briefly. I have also noticed there are snack foods which simply don't work as fodder for inventiveness. Peanut butter never works regardless of the quality of cracker. Nothing milk-based works, not even Haagen Dazs ice cream. There is no temptation to chocolate or cookies of any brand. Cheddar cheese, the only cheese I ever eat, appeals even less than usual. Little O'Henry bars, Halloween size, are good for one injection of inspiration but then completely lose their value. Although I am fond of yogurt slurpies with frozen mixed berries as a meal, they have no motivational value.

The only beverage that finds its way on to my stone coaster engraved with HOPE is green tea. It takes most of the day to sip my way to the dregs and only then can I witness the encouragement through the glass-bottomed cup. Perhaps the relationship between eating and writing shall remain a mystery to me. Perhaps having quirks and cravings is just one of the pitfalls of living life as a writer.

Clothing the author

Ever try to write in the nude?

Doesn't work for me. My office is near our front door. I get cold easily, my grandmother wouldn't approve, and it puzzles the dog. Nude is too extreme. Writing in my dressing gown or pajamas seems to keep my mind asleep. I can't write in my bathing suit at a resort, yet I am quite successful doing so if I am fully clothed. Go figure.

Equally inhibiting for me is the professional uniform of my former academic life. Uncomfortable shoes, panty hose biting into my waist, a suit jacket binding my shoulders, a blouse with tight cuffs restricting my wrists, a skirt preventing me from reclining with my feet on the desk, are all counter-indications for writing. I used to take a sports bag to work so that once the day's commitments were over I could shed the restrictions of the body and don a sweat suit. I would love to say it was a designer version, but it wasn't.

It seems that my *writer* is embodied. She has to be able to feel. She has to be able to move. She needs to be room temperature, not too hot, not too cold. She needs a type of freedom that comes with being physically unencumbered. Not scruffy though, like painting clothes. Not shorts. Don't know why. Preferably color coordinated. Don't know why. Preferably not black. No watch. No jewelry except my wedding band. My favorite apparel is a loose pant with a draw-string waist, and a t-shirt or loose sweatshirt, depending on the weather. Never a bra. Thick socks and supportive tennis shoes. No make up.

Susan Musgrave in her essay *Women Over the PreSchool Age* in the book *I Feel Great about My Hands* says, "One of the highlights of the writing life is that every time you sit down to start work on a new book, you don't have to go shopping first for a new wardrobe. As long as you work at home, you don't even need to dress respectably."

Does someone who writes romance novels dress differently than a person who writes science fiction? Does the author of a history text wear apparel that varies from the poet?

When I write my first comedy, I wonder what I will wear?

Writing in the night

That wonderful flow of writing that the night invites has none of the pathology Alice Flaherty speaks of in *The Midnight Disease*. The stream of words rise up from a warm geyser, not in compulsive hypergraphia but as an offering of the mystery of the not visible, of the not heard in the chaos of the day.

There is such gentleness to the night. There is something different about writing in the hours after dusk. Perhaps it is that the world has withdrawn from me rather than I must withdraw from the world. The furnace clicks in and out on occasion. Even the dog is asleep. On occasion, the moon keeps me company but tonight the outer world is pitch black. It is the kind of night a photographer loves for *painting with light*. The silence is unbroken with television or music. Nibbling from a bowl of medjool dates beside me keeps my blood sugar up. How different are these nights than the long ones beside dad's bedside only months ago.

Even as handmaiden to death, when I wrote once or twice on those nights, I felt the quiet of solitude, the realities of simple living. Those nights were long and draining and yet a privilege.

I remember the first night I ever wrote throughout the night. The ending of a manuscript was within reach, yet there was no compulsion. The writing simply had a life of its own. Green tea to drink. Macaroons to snack on. There was no low point. No point where I felt I should pack it in. No restless moments where the fridge or the television seduced me out of my writer's coma. It was as if no external distractions invited no internal distractions.

There was just the night, the words, and me. The words simply flowed. The ideas came easily. There was no editing or reflection. The internal critic slumbered. Then the sun began to light the landscape. I was in awe of the timelessness. Ah, for those rare episodes of timeless hours.

Seeing without the words

In search of frivolous viewing, like the serendipity
I have come to expect, my thumb quit pressing
the channel changer when I landed on the CBC
documentary, *Beyond Words: Photographers of
War*, a compelling commentary on the boldness with
which some people live life as part of making visual,
often haunting, testimonies of the state of humanity.
I yearn for the bolts of adrenalin they report are part
of capturing images of life first hand.

There is a directness to photography that writing
cannot access. It is one thing to report violence in the
streets. It is another to film a soccer match played
with the decapitated head of a young dissident. Such
photographs are never published. Like manuscripts,
their photographs are subject to editing and/or
rejection based on market appeal.

When I go armed to events with my camera, I
am not uncommonly accused of or asked if I am

missing the activity with my eye so perpetually in the viewfinder. I never feel I am. The lens I choose and the angles I shoot provide a satisfaction that the panorama encompassed by my natural eye cannot provide as it must grapple with the entire gestalt.

Photography allows the sense that we recall, not the days, but the moments. It has an immediacy. A moment's hesitation can mean the image will remain forever only a memory. There will be no confirming document. With writing that is always true. Words on paper have no truth other than the truth I attach to them. Can words ever capture more powerfully than a picture, the complexity and intensity of a mother's embrace as she is reunited with her child, alive, in the aftermath of the tsunami? Is my camera in some way, a writing tool?

I am pulled by both mediums. There are times, when I ache for a photograph to deepen my writing. At other times, I ache for the words to interpret an image. With writing, there is always a cerebral interloper, a cognitive processing. Even if the writing is highly evocative, it must be read, the words must make sense. With a photograph the language is more primordial, the response more immediate and visceral. How will these two languages co-exist in my life as a writer?

Choosing the form of expression

In my youth, no one ever said you could grow up and be a photographer. Had they, my life might well have taken a very different turn. From the time I got my first Brownie Starflash at age ten until today with my single reflex digital Canon D60, my love of photography has never waned.

I loved writing, but not with the passion of photography. I was vaguely aware that one could go to Ryerson Institute for journalism, and the thought crossed my mind fleetingly. I didn't know a single professional photographer or published writer. Neither vocation was ever featured on career day! Photography was something one did as a hobby. Writing was something impoverished waiters, the independently wealthy, or people who worked for newspapers did.

For years, my writing and photography seemed like separate activities. At some point, they began to blend together in a seamless voice. Writer and photographer. Not writer or photographer. Both captured mood, both captured moments. Both had something to say, often complementing each other. Sometimes, the image hungered for words. Sometimes the words cried out for a picture.

Why then 'life as a writer'? Why not life as a photographer? Or life as an artist combining both? I have not been able to answer that question even for myself. I cannot give up either, yet I feel identity requires a choice. To attempt both would be to ensure mediocrity in both. One must be the main course; the other becomes a side dish.

Both say something about me. There is a truth in Freeman Paterson's words, "The lens shoots both directions." Some of my most satisfying writing times involve placing a photo that I have taken on a small easel in front of me and waiting for the photograph to speak. Waiting for the image to inform me. Not forcing meaning. Just waiting, listening in silence, until a voice comes forward.

What I photograph, I believe is no accident. When I allow the photograph to speak, it confirms the truth of the Latin expression "Nisi in intellect sed pruis in sensibus". Translated it means, "Nothing comes into the mind that does not first come through the senses." I need to trust that my eye is a powerful conduit for what I need to attend to in life, a lens to show me how to be free.

Fitting in the fitness

Someone ought to write a book about fitness for writers. We sit. We sit a lot. We sit more than therapists. We can slouch though or move to the picnic table if we want. Depending on the arrangements in our writing spaces, we don't even need to move to print our drafts. Writer's health isn't news-worthy. You never see headlines that say "Writers at risk for ..." Not because we are not at risk but because, who cares?

I have simply not seen a research study of the mental and/or physical health of writers. I simply do not know how I compare to the health of those who also call themselves writers. Are we as a group, fitness challenged?

My writing space is less than what is ergonomically recommended, my life style often verges on sedentary, and my passion tends to be spent in front of a key board, despite having more time than when I lived a

24/7 life in the fast lane. There is little energy left for training for a marathon.

If I am not careful, I get what I call scholar's collar, that humped over, slouched down look that comes from spending hours in basically one position. My back can get cranky if I am not careful. My experiment with sitting on a large blue ball to ensure proper posture while typing ended with me toppling into the paper shredder with Molly licking my face.

I seem plagued with experimenting. I resolve to walk a mile a day before writing. It doesn't happen. I resolve to weight lift three times a week. It doesn't happen. It would be more accurate to say it doesn't happen when I have a writing project on the go. Despite no deadlines, I opt for writing rather than sweating! I don't need deadlines or threats to get myself to the computer. The same doesn't seem true in terms of getting myself to the treadmill. If I was as committed to writing as I am about my physical fitness I would never get any publications completed.

One physical exception was committing myself to a seven day camping trip in a solo kayak in the Sea of Cortez. I was motivated. I did not want to be the weakest link of the four of us on the adventure.

When it comes to writing, there is always an exciting manuscript to create. With fitness, I simply need a comparable excitation.

Releasing the therapist

Because living my life as a writer is now in the foreground, and living my life as a therapist is in the background, it doesn't mean I will quit listening, quit hearing the pain, quit being curious about how people make their lives difficult. In many ways, therapists co-author lives rather than books. In both roles, I am more perceptive when I am free to simply observe, to forego the dance of interpretation done at the altar of helpfulness and to not concern myself about whether change occurs. I need to be free to choose my own lines and speak my own truth while deeply respecting that we must each "author" our own lives, figure out who the other characters are and weave a story that makes sense to us. We each hold the stylus to scribe our own lives.

Both of us, the writer and the therapist, likely share curiosities: Tell me about Mark. Help me understand that encounter. How did you know your sister was upset? Who else was present? What happened first, and when? What was the darkest moment of the episode? What did you do under those circumstances? Was hope a friend or foe in this case? How might it have been different if Mark had been away? Who would tell this story differently? What has changed since it happened? How will you tell the story differently in a decade? With each question, the kaleidoscope shifts, the understanding changes. As a writer, there is no standard of psychological wellness guiding conversation, no diagnosis to deliver, no treatment to administer.

As a therapist I am bound to a culture of niceness that we call ethics. My intent must always be constructive. The story line cannot change simply to entertain me.

As a writer, the characters need not sit across from me. I get to invent them, composites of my own life encounters. I can dismiss or exalt them, praise or punish them, all with the stroke of a pen.

Releasing the therapist, while accepting the writer, is a difficult and slow process, but they will always be close friends.

Listening for the Inspiration

I remind myself every morning: Nothing I say this day will teach me anything. So if I'm going to learn, I must do it by listening.

Larry King

Too often we underestimate the power of a touch, a smile, a kind word, a listening ear, an honest compliment, or the smallest act of caring, all of which have the potential to turn a life around.

Leo Buscaglia

Lamenting a dying craft

I loved her from the moment I heard her Polish accent over the phone. Our first encounter was around her translating some writing of mine for a psychiatrist friend of hers in Poland. When she arrived with her two dogs, it took only moments to know there was something rare about her. Her every statement was animated. Her very being was passionate. About everything. About literature. About young people. About the Bread of Life project she runs to support an orphanage. About the lecture series she single handedly sustained for years.

A visit to her studio took me back a hundred years. As the only archival bookbinder in Western Canada, Ksenia kept alive a dying art form, a beautiful but dying art form. The smell of the leather hanging from the wall beams is stronger than the herbal tea that is brewing behind the work bench. Samples of her work dot the shelves, while her aging canine companions occupy the better part of the old hardwood floor. Icons of her Catholic heritage are here and there. The genuine exuberance of her greeting has me already thinking of when I will visit again.

Seated across from her she turns her computer screen to show me sample after sample of book covers, one and only book covers. She has already shown me how she stitches the pages in a way that makes me think of the era of Dickens. She speaks to me of hope, her words mix hope and despair as she thinks of aging alone in this country and of not knowing what she will do when there is no demand for her skills, the skills of an artisan that take a lifetime to perfect.

I imagined having Ksenia hand bind one or more of my volumes. I fantasized a benefactor promoting her work through some as yet unknown channel. Having a book bound in this way would place it among the tradition of treasured literature. It will likely never happen though. Like so many of our artisans, she has closed her doors and returned to her Poland. She has taken with her a rare knowledge, and we are as writers the poorer for it.

Reading about writing

What a joy to read a writer who has me smiling, thinking, and distressed, all in three pages. *Thank You for Not Reading* by Dubravka Ugresic gets a 10! For several years, I have been a restless reader. When asked what I wanted for a retirement gift, I requested a list of recommendations for reading. Among the heart warming gifts was a 'here is your career' in a scrapbook, including people's suggestions for my reading. So far, I haven't read a single referral – but I intend to.

Ugresic's crisp readable essays make me want to meet her, to know if she is short and dark or tall and angular. She reminds us that in American culture "the author's appearance in wide-circulation newspapers and TV is more important than what the author has actually written". With humor, with pathos, and with fiction, she brings to light the commercial nature of writing in a way that is both refreshing and discouraging. The litany of "how to write" books she cites would be the envy of any novice who believes if I just learn something more, just practice this or that, just meet him or her, just go to one more workshop, I will PUBLISH!

As a novice psychologist, I recall not only purchasing but reading every text and trade book I could afford. No pathology would be outside my domain of understanding and few outside of my expertise. The benefit of my compulsion came from the eventual realization that my interest was in potential rather than in pathology. Pathology simply did not explain the remarkable people facing adversity with courage that I was meeting. Protocols for assessments and empirically validated treatments would not guide my life as a psychologist.

Having digested many of the 'how to" books about writing, I notice that the process is somewhat similar. Just as I was not interested in a directory of psychological disorders, the volumes diagnosing grammar, addressing genres, and discussing the marketing of writing have been sidelined early to make way for my own development as a writer.

Writing like an elder

It is hard to estimate Ella's age. I suspect she is nearly seventy. There are gray hairs, extra pounds, and some edema obvious under the ankle socks nestled in Birkenstocks. The accoutrements of her youth simply melt into the wisdom of her persona. There is no disguise necessary once we understand who we are.

When Ella speaks, the world feels safer. The quality of her voice speaks to the years of digging deeply into the pool of pain and being willing to retrieve a dipper of refreshing thought. Resentment, if she had any, was never given a place to root in her heart. Single mom to six, her 360 square foot senior's suite is like the command station for a missile launch. Boxes here. Papers there, yet not disheveled. Everything is functional, not fussy like my grandmother who had starched doilies on her tea wagon. The missile she is launching will land in Africa, with immeasurable influence.

She won her first poetry contest at eight and hasn't stopped writing since. Poetry, story, essays, letters. This month it's a well-crafted letter to her aging network to raise awareness of the plight of African grandmothers who find themselves mourning children and adopting grandchildren. Her style is invitational, not imposing. She relays the nature of her personal commitment and invites others to identify theirs.

On Sundays, she bakes cookies and wraps them to meet the public health standards needed to donate them to the soup kitchen. A small smile creeps onto her face, while her eyes twinkle with a declaration that it excuses her from attending church. Each cookie, she says, is a prayer for the person who consumes it. Each one is made with love with the best available ingredients. Nothing is asked in return. Simple. Sincere.

What if I could approach my writing that way? What if I thought of my words as a gift to an unknown reader who may be nourished by them. That would mean that there couldn't be, wouldn't be, any unhealthy ingredients or filler. Every word would be added because it was needed. Every thought would be wholesome in its intent.

How then would I write about pain? I will go lightly on sweetness and flavor my writing mostly with meaning, beauty, and, on occasion, perhaps even with a measure of pain.

Noticing the power of the pen

It is said that the pen is mightier than the sword. Really? Then why are we not boosting financial support for authors rather than retrofitting helicopters, sending young men and women to writing studios rather than deploying them to the theatre of war, arming every gang member with a personal journal, equipping every young person with inspiration rather than increasing tuition fees?

For those we feel we must liberate, how would the cost of equipping them with literacy compare to the cost of a new fleet? Why is there a greater market for illegal weapons than for books? Why is forbidden nuclear material a more profitable enterprise than banned books? There is no end to what cries out to be examined critically. The arguments are endless, with truth partially represented in all perspectives.

Writers are influential. Despite electronic media, it is a writer who frames the news, a speech writer who crafts public opinion, an essayist who asks us to think, a novelist who puts us into the adventure. The level of exposure of any writer to readership is, however, not solely under his or her control.

John Boyko's relatively obscure book *Into the Hurricane* documents the media contribution to fear-based political coverage in the printed word. Changes in the publishing world keep restricted-audience books and small presses on the lower shelves, relegating higher profile books and major presses to the upper shelves. For informed controversy to wield its power, it likely needs to be associated with a celebrity.

What about outside the public arena? There is the power of that dying art form - the personal letter, that dying art form that can keep distant romance alive for months or crush it in an instant. Nothing so warms my heart as an honest to goodness letter with a stamp on it. An e-mail update dispensed to multiple recipients falls short of what I would call personal correspondence.

The ultimate power of the written word extends even into death. The reading of a will can feel like the shot that rang through a family. Forgiveness or revenge. Gratitude or being passed over. Those unemotional legalese words are powerful!

Writing to make sense

Dear Dana:

I am out at a place called Rundle's Mission, a retreat center. It is the site of the first Protestant mission in Alberta. There is an old log lodge and two houses, each with five bedrooms, a kitchen, a large living room and dining room area. It needs new rugs, new couches and some new wall hangings. When you sit on the couch, you feel like you might disappear, the years have so worn out its springs. Staying here overnight though is only $20. People come here to attend workshops and just to get away.

I am getting away from the phone, the family, the fax machine, and the fridge in order to have some quiet time as a writer. More and more these days I am living my life as a writer. I am of course still a psychologist, a step mom, a foster mom, an auntie, a sister, a wife, and a dog owner. The difference is that writing will be an increasingly important part of my life rather than just something I try to do if I have a little time. I am not sure what I will write yet but that seems less important than the commitment to the writing.

You keep coming to mind while I am here. I continue to recall the sincerity with which you approached learning to journal when you encountered the dilemma of relationship bullying. Your words of some months later, "My journal is where I go to become the person I want to be", have never left me. In them is a gem of wisdom that will nurture you all of your life.

In many ways, I hurt that you had to wrestle with injustice so early in your life. Nor have I forgotten *Dana Day* when you received the first of your great grandmother's teacups. In the years to come may the journal that you also received that day, and quiet time on occasion, perhaps even on a regular basis, help you with the inevitable chaos and clutter of life. When you write, you have a means of making sense of your world.

You become an observer to your own experience. You step out of the scene and see things differently. In so doing, you grow.

Envisioning a prison

"There is only one point to writing It allows you to do the impossible. Writing makes sorrow endurable, evil intelligible, justice desirable and love possible."

Roger Rosenblatt (2012): Kayak Morning.
New York: Harper Collins, p. 127

I have a dream. That every female in this institution, offender or employee, would write a piece that they feel good about. That every person would come to know they can 'author' their own life, despite circumstances. That every woman would experiment with writing, would come to understand that it is not about good spelling and grammar. It is about knowing and believing in ourselves. It is about building community in a culture of pain and punishment.

I have a dream that the pain could go on paper rather than be carved into her own flesh, or numbed by medication, legal or illegal. I have a dream we would find a way of speaking our truth to ourselves, to those we hurt and those who hurt us; and to those who imprison us, including ourselves.

I have a dream each woman writer will recognize the longing of another and gently encourage her to also find her voice and that we will become a collective voice, not of rebellion and advocacy, but of change at its deepest level. That with your writings, whether they be vignettes, or poetry, or starter novels - that you can craft a community of concern with your writing such that every incarcerated women has at least a chance to someday say, "I can 'Be here, Be myself, and Be hopeful'."

I have a dream that every woman released from this institution will know her life story and have no shame, despite regret. That she will feel equipped to write her next chapter, that she will choose her co-authors well. That those responsible for custody will write to develop themselves as characters who are instruments of humanity.

I know that when I leave here, you cannot. Yet, I know of many situations where incarcerated people found a way of not only surviving but found ways of finding meaning while held in captivity, fairly or unfairly.

Inspired by the Edmonton Institute for Women
Writing Group, August 2003

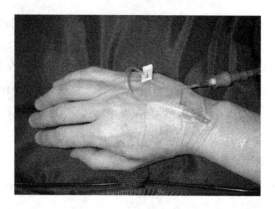

Wrestling with the "what if"

When I meet colleagues and friends who continue to be in the world of day timers and deadlines as a way of staving off the pain of what they fear will be long dull days in retirement, I am at a loss as to what to say. I didn't retire from; I retired to. For me, retirement means the freedom to write. Even more specifically, it means the freedom to write what appeals to me at any given time. I can literally write what I want, and I can write when I want. How could someone not want that privilege?

I have convinced myself even confinement to a senior's home where the only accoutrements might be a toothbrush, an afghan and a deaf roommate would be more than tolerable as long as I have access to any equivalent of quill and parchment. As long as words could transfer from my inner life into text, I would continue to feel alive. Life would have some acceptable version of meaning. There is no fear that one day I might rise with nothing to draw me to my craft. If I were granted life sufficient to address only the projects that I presently can envision, I would have to apply for an extension to the normal life span in order to complete them.

The fear I harbor and rarely allow myself to approach is the "what if" of my physical abilities. Every three months, I come to the Out Patient Department for my intravenous osteoporosis treatment. Now that I am out of the fracture range, the fate that literally lurks in my bones seems distant. My skeletal system is not the only threat. With my dietary anomalies, internment in a dwelling with conventional meals would be tantamount to imprisonment on death row.

What if for some unknown reason, I could no longer get my B12 or Vitamin D shots, and I began to waste again? What if I become malnourished and the creativity waned to the extreme? What if my hands or shoulders could not endure the mechanical tasks of writing? What if, despite presently decent eyesight, blindness stole the very gift that facilitates me observing the world? Deafness seems for some reason a lesser evil. Locked in a silent world feels less intimidating than destined to a dark one. Can people write if they lose their senses?

In preparation, perhaps I will write myself into courage.

Capturing the moment

Today I tried to write one of the *tea stories*. The details have slipped away. Somehow I thought I would never forget the formal tea with a 90-year-old wonderfully wise elder and an eight year old, both diabetics. We had tea in Elise's room at the seniors' home. At that time, she resided in the west wing that provided meals and basic nursing assistance. I can recall the old sewing machine in the corner but not where the television was. I can recall the blandness of the walls but not the texture of the rug. I can vaguely remember the clutter of photographs on an old dresser. I can't though feel what I remember seeing in Hilary's eyes as it registered that this really, really, old woman has diabetes too. I couldn't recall just what it was that Elise said that put Hilary at ease.

    I couldn't recall what kind of tea we had or whether I had brought in a flower for the center of the tablecloth. I do recall, I brought in a white linen cloth. That I remember. I don't remember what I brought for us to eat that was diabetic friendly. I don't recall what day of the week it was. Saturday, I think. Maybe Friday. I know it was in the summer holidays. Perhaps it isn't important. As a writer, I could just fill in all the details. Somehow though, I wanted to recall the real thing.

I keep a journal next to my bed and often carry one when I travel. I have even removed myself briefly from a dinner party to record a writing idea.

Sadly, I usually let the day seduce me away from recording observations and experience which means, for the most part, they are lost forever. Similarly with dreams, in an early morning journal entry I jotted, "Molly (our dog) was trying to help. She caught two rats". To this day, these words remain insufficient to bring back what I thought was a vivid and unforgettable dream. I was convinced I would not forget the context of the dream.

Time has taught me that it is nearly impossible to hold a thought until dawn. As Sheila Bender in *Keeping a Journal You Love* says of these sparks, "They're pretty, but you couldn't cook with them." To live my life as a writer, it is not enough to notice life. I need to find a way of noticing how it is recorded in my senses.

Being politically correct

Academia is a political arena. Step on the wrong toes, publicly support an unpopular cause, and watch the subtle pressure begin to be applied. Doors close. Funding is suddenly not accessible. Invitations to speak at conferences disappear. Now outside of academia, I relish the freedom I have to write about topics of my choice in my own tone of voice.

In academia, an author is subject to forces that pay lip service to intellectual freedom while rewarding traditional content and genres. In recent years, reporting research results that were contrary to government views was virtually forbidden. Thankfully, this policy has now been reversed. There is though, a different, subtle pressure within academia to adhere to a formula for inquiry and hence, an inferred formula for writing.

The issue is one of power. The defining marker is the privileging of one paradigm, that of the conventional research model, characterized by the quantification of almost everything. There are important questions that cannot be answered with numbers. Thank goodness for those who risk exploring outside of the box, challenging mainstream thought with inquiry and writing of a wholly different nature. By doing so, they dent the cookie cutter templates of scientific writing, inviting us to a world of informed opinion and deep reflection. Neither writing style is right nor wrong. The challenge is to come to our work with conviction and to write with courage. Not to do so is also a political statement. We speak with our silence.

Who we hang out with affects our writing. No wonder many writers hold up in offices and writing studios and cubbyholes away from the mentors of mediocrity. Away from institutional structures that punish innovative thought. They seek a retreat where they can craft their influence with ideas and words that are less censored. It begs the question, "What am I risking with my writing?"

Preparing to Write

Give me six hours to chop down a tree and I will spend the first four sharpening the axe.

Abraham Lincoln

He who is best prepared can best serve his moment of inspiration.

Samuel Taylor Coleridge

Choosing not to quilt

Walking through a quilting store today sparked a twinge of sadness that life is not sufficiently long enough to inhale, with zeal, all of the life experiences to which I am drawn. Committing myself to writing means that there are other things I won't be doing. Except in small and amateur doses, I won't be quilting, golfing, training for the upcoming Master's games, sewing my own clothes, mastering Norwegian, pursuing cake decorating, or learning to do breathtaking flower arrangements. As I see it, in life there is room for one major and perhaps one minor additional passion, embraced at the risk of diluting a focused life, a life with an organizing principle. In my case, writing. Photography and kayaking have already claimed two of the available supplementary slots.

Choice is a mandatory requirement of living life intentionally, rather than as a response to random opportunity. Even as a writer, I must choose what to write, for what audience (if any), in what genre. I must choose how well read to be and how to sustain an inner life while living in an over-stimulated culture.

Giving up things is not in me. The necessary but dull voice of maturity has so far convinced me that the trip across Sweden on a dog sled that was to be my retirement adventure may be out of reach given the aftermath of a motor vehicle accident. My longstanding desire to spend time in India and Africa are held at bay with the realities of a high risk health condition. Even choosing a good night's sleep rather than a forty-mile drive to see the latest hit movie is sometimes difficult. Pursuing activity though is not the same as savoring the events that nourish my depth and creativity. Gluttony is not my friend as a writer.

May I learn to discern when distraction can be wisely welcomed. May spontaneity and discipline find a rightful balance. May I learn to meet solitude with steadfastness, to invite quiet where chaos might encroach. May I one day declare with confidence that "it was good to be a writer," not because of what I wrote but because of what it demanded of me.

Living up to my word

I would like to be fit without exercising. I would like to eat cheesecake and be slim. I would like to be adventuresome without leaving home. I would like to be learned without reading the Great Books series. I would love to be a chef without having to shop for groceries. I would love to entertain without having to do the dishes.

I would like to do my craft without revisiting grammar and punctuation rules once in a while. Ironically friends and colleagues would describe me as disciplined. In other words, I can make it happen. I just haven't found a way to like being disciplined. What helps?

Rewards don't work that well with me. I have tried the "if/then" game often. If I accomplish this, then I get this or that. If I work this long, then I get to do something else for that long. Goals do help. In the end though, it is my word that counts. My word is important to me, even when it is my word to myself. I am careful to set realistic goals. I may decide to have a draft by Friday. Maybe I have to burn the midnight oil two nights to make it happen. That works better for me than "I will write three hours every morning."

I have to be careful to include goals as the writing nears completion. I am what I call an 80%/20% person. Once 80% of the task is complete my interest wanes. That last 20% is the dull stuff. The editing stuff. The book proposal stuff. The agent stuff. The publisher stuff.

It helps to tell others a version of my goal. Not too many people. Not too explicitly. That is, I try not to talk about the content of the writing too much, just the end goal.

At one level, I don't really care what others think. At another level, I guess I must. I certainly have a thing about living up to my commitments. If I say I will do something, then I will do it.

Some of those things that we learn as children may have a touch of pathology, but they have their value as well. Being taught that my word means a lot, is one of those essential values that, in the end, spells out integrity.

Assigning a writing space

Not every one has the privilege of a writing studio, a room of his or her own for the purpose of creating masterpieces. J.K. Rowling is said to have written *Harry Potter* with a toddler at her feet in a local restaurant. Novels were written in filthy trenches. People create while sitting in beds, on boats, on makeshift tables, and while they watch their daughters play soccer. Some insist that writing can happen anywhere, anytime. Others say blocks of time are mandatory.

Jill Krementz in *The Writer's Desk* gives us a peek at the writing spaces of recognized authors. From meticulous to messy, from formal to bohemian, from simple to chaotic, there seems to be no formula. Some are small, some spacious, some ordered, some cluttered. Some have feline and canine companions. Most seem to be occupied solely by the author.

If I could design my writing space, it would have a multitude of shelves, liberal filing space, be flooded with light, and have ample options for laying out data and documents. It would have only a couple of reminders of another life with a clear avoidance of knickknacks to dust and distract.

I am growing into my writing space. I now use a different computer in another space for recipes and e-mails. On my day of private practice, I think of my clients as co-authors coming to write the next chapter of their lives. My writing stole hangs on a bronze hook. I wonder sometimes why I don't wear it more often. The sheepskin on my chair adds an earthy flavor, and my Buddha board reminds me the challenge is endless. My one black and white photo perpetually inspires me.

Outside, we have a small hermitage that could be winterized and adapted. That way I would be almost secluded. It isn't seclusion I need. It is time, and light, and focus. I still need to create the internal writing space, the place where I am willing to go, the place where writing comes first. The place where words can feel at home. No physical writing space will ensure I write. That comes from a writing space of a different kind.

Rearranging the office

It had been weeks since my fingers had touched the keyboard. Even the notebook I carried around in hopes of a few moments of silence remained empty.

Hospital cafeterias and doctors' offices provided the occasional quiet times. Somehow though, I didn't want to put words to the uncertainty that was the reality of our lives. I took the precious moments of silence to just sit. Not to ruminate. Not to worry. Just to sit. There was no raw need to write myself into or out of fear.

I never stopped feeling like a writer. However, being a wife, being a friend, being present at the bedside felt more important. Writing memories to our souls was the first order of each day.

It wasn't possible to plan for the day. Now that the intensity has passed and life is returning to some stability, I expected to return to the keyboard.

Instead, on my first day back, it was not text that I edited but the office itself. If I could not control death and destiny, I could put order into my daily existence.

Without conscious thought, the psychology books were coming off the shelves. The library downstairs was being rearranged, and the remainder of the writing books were coming upstairs.

One grouping was the journal writing references, another section was for the writing prompts. Authors who write about writing took another shelf. Grammatical references took yet another spot. One filing drawer was for the current projects. One for ideas. Yet another one for the remnants of my academic life.

Two days passed. Every paper in the office was reviewed, discarded, or filed. The overflowing wicker basket of filing now stood empty. A day later I was writing again. Something more than my office was purged. The words are flowing again.

It is like the words knew when I was ready. They knew what it would take to ready me. They didn't abandon me. They just waited patiently while life diverted me. Needed me. They knew the homecoming would come at it's own pace.

I recognize the pattern. For me, order precedes productivity. The author within doesn't like chaos. I can write about chaos but not in chaos.

Splitting infinitives

At the prison, I joked about the grammar guards and the punctuation police when the women in my writing class worried about the mechanics of writing. Yet, I also find myself wondering on many occasions, is it "is" or "are"; is it phenomena or phenomenon, data or datum? Is it a hyphen or a semi-colon? Is it "that" or "which"? Have I split the infinitive – again?

As a student, I actually liked grammar. I liked naming the parts of a sentence and identifying a clause as principle or subordinate. In university, I loved linguistics. For me, it was like mathematics. There was an underlying structure to it and, like spelling, a multitude of exceptions.

I consult my trusty *Grammar Desk Reference* regularly, as it seems beyond me to master the rules of the use of quotations. As for remembering the protocol for referencing, I now have evidence that short-term memory goes first! After years of exposure to APA style, I cannot account for the fact that I still can't recall with certainty which comes first – the publisher or the city of publication.

One of the differences between being a professor and living life as a writer is that there is no longer a graduate student standing by obliged to proof read or re-do references as part of their meager livelihood. I appreciate the computer spell and grammar check, but don't always agree with it. It also doesn't catch a meaningless word if it is spelled correctly. I have discovered that often neither do I. I tend to read what I think I have written, particularly after the second or third draft. Reading out loud is almost the only way I catch missed words and clumsy wording. Having been a reviewer of submitted manuscripts, I am sensitive to impressions made by a poorly constructed cover letter and frequent slips in spelling. Somehow the quality of other things then come into question.

Language also changes. What was "right" when grammar was taught in my day may now be stuffy. It isn't likely that my memory will improve, that language will become static, or that computers will approximate perfection. Seems to me that it is just part of the craft, like a carpenter who must constantly check the sharpness of his saw blade, like a sculptor who brings life to stone.

Selecting my writing tool

I am caught between generations. Penmanship was once an art. Every student was schooled in the craft of putting words onto paper in a legible manner, artistic enough that years later they might be read by a grandchild who would say, "Wow, look at grandpa's handwriting." There was a sense of script to it. Steve, my Irish colleague, each year taught the grade seven boys to write much like calligraphers. I suspect to this day that they are grateful for the skill. It turned adolescents' messy pages into rather deceivingly scholarly appearing documents. I can't vouch for the content being similarly improved.

My generation can make a computer keyboard sing but not all of us can think while doing so. There is still, for me, something about a fountain pen that makes a letter a real letter. There is something about receiving a letter handwritten by someone who intended it specifically for me. Xeroxed Christmas letters have their place and perhaps even e-mails that are copied to a dozen or more friends serve a purpose. They don't, however, serve the purpose of an intimate relationship with the recipient.

There is something about a dozen sharpened HB pencils, not too short. I love using them until dull and then selecting the next one. It is like lining up a dozen nails and hammering them in a sequence. Somehow, the used pencils signal progress. Eversharps with 5mm leads provide evidence as well. Every time I click to bring down more lead, it means I have been writing.

The real difference though is in the feel. On the computer, my fingers work cooperatively but of necessity, independently, to record my thoughts. A fountain pen has a feel to it. A pencil has a feel to it. An eversharp has a certain feel to it. My whole hand, my whole arm feels the movement. The connection between mind and hand is different. The computer screen is different than the lined writing pad that I use for long hand. A younger writer or a more seasoned writer on a computer may feel differently. Until there is a shift for me, poetry at least will still be done longhand.

Wanting to write is not enough

I wanna' be a writer. I have no children to mourn my passing. No legacy to leave besides the few words of wisdom that the decades have carved into my character.

I don't want to be a quilter, a dog trainer, an extreme athlete, a chef, or a doting grandmother. I am too far past my prime to climb mountains. Too deaf to start music lessons. Too lazy to start a business. Too tired, or is it too selfish, to be a volunteer for one more worthy cause.

I want to sit with myself unencumbered with obligation. I want to be a pampered writer. I want my meals to appear, my clothes to wash themselves, my bills to be on automatic withdrawal. I want to stay fit but exercise without exertion.

And yes, of course, I would prefer fame to obscurity. I relish the fantasy of book blurbs replete with glowing reviews. And book tours packed with the illusion of importance. And media coverage full of silly questions to which there are no answers. I have been there before. It was fun and it is fodder for those years ahead when I will rise on schedule if I want morning porridge in the dining room with others who have been assigned to insignificance.

But today, I need to carve out three hours and patiently wait in the stillness for the quiet voice of the muse. I need to welcome the words that come from that place of deep and quiet courage. The words that speak to what it means to become human, the words that open the heart to wrestle with the unspoken questions that we collude to avoid.

I need to understand that I am a writer and my task is to find the words that express the unspoken questions.

Just what is this task? The more I craft my ideas into essays, stories, poems, and books, the more I realize that my task is to simply observe, not to entertain. My task is to reflect, not to instruct. I want to invite my reader to that central question, "What is it to be human?". My task is to invite my reader to join me in that reflection.

Learning to notice

Children watch everything. They notice everything. They are present to all that they encounter. They judge with their senses. If it smells bad, they turn away. If it tastes bad, they spit it out. If it is scary, they close their eyes. If it is smooth, they put their cheek to it. If it is too loud, they clasp their hands over their ears and look with puzzlement to the adult who is supposed to protect them. If something is still, they may mirror the stillness. If something is funny, they may giggle with delight. When something bores them, they move on. When something fascinates them, they remain fixed on it.

As we grow older, we notice less. A subtle censor slips into how we experience our world. We develop preferences and prematurely reject what we name as *not interesting*. Soon we have entered into the numbness of mediocrity. We delight in less. We miss the tones of red in the autumn leaves.

We miss the flute in the background of the symphony. We interpret and analyze and dull the world.

When I read Mary Oliver's poems, I am acutely aware that she not only observed the world of nature, she felt the texture of the wind, heard the call of the lune. She noticed everything.

I want to notice. I don't have to go anywhere to notice. I need to be present to the world I live in. In my world, there is a prairie wind.

> Prairie wind
> So dry the wings of butterflies need vaseline
> So cold the wolverines huddle together
> So strong the buffalo stand still
> So welcome in the scorching sun
> So persistent the oak leans as it ages.
>
> Prairie wind
> That soothes a summer picnic
> That refreshes the sweating farmer
> Prairie wind that howls at night
> That whispers through forests
> That eagles use to soar.

To be a writer, I need to feel and taste and touch and hear the world. It doesn't matter whether I like what I experience.

Inviting the Muse

The idea of the Muse has been around since at least 800 BC. In *The Odyssey*, Homer prays for the Invocation of the Muse ending with "Make the tale live for us in all its many bearings, O Muse." Stephen King, in *On Writing*, wrote, "Your job is to make sure the muse knows where you're going to be every day from nine 'til noon. Or seven 'til three, …If he does know, I assure you that sooner or later he'll start showing up." There are those who believe that to be a real poet:

I have to sit under a birch tree,
    and sip brandy,
    and have bare feet,
    and watch the swans
    take flight,
    as I wait for the Muse.

So maybe I can only be a poet
    if I have a pasture,
    and a pond, and
    it's October.
    I can feel ready to write,
    and still, something is missing.
    I'm ready to write!
    My pencils are sharpened.
    The cell phone is off.
    There's a two-hour stash
    of dates and cashews,
    for those moments when
    I need to pause for inspiration,
    or to consult my thesaurus.

I am ready to write.
    Poetic lines are bouncing,
    like golf balls
    on an asphalt highway,
    destined to roll into a culvert.
    I must write, or
    the words will be lost forever.

What's missing? I need to let the clutter of life slip into the background. I need to feel the "still point" that is, for me, a forerunner to the flow of words to come. I need to be present, to myself and to my purpose. I need to be open to the Muse AND be ready to work. Whether you believe in the muse or not, she doesn't type.

Finding the Feeling

The river is everywhere.

Herman Hesse: Siddharta

Showing up is important

Some mornings I don't feel like writing. Having awakened groggy, there is a temptation to veg out watching Canada AM. Molly is asleep on her dog bed having gotten me up at 3 a.m., not returning to the door despite my 20-minute wait at the door! If I could growl at her, I would. Hours later, looking at the clock, it is necessary to ask myself, "Am I committed to this or not?" At least I can dress unconcerned about public image while I sip the hot lemon drink that Allen brings to my bedside each morning to ease me into the day.

My commitment is to begin at 9:15, a play on starting a writer's life on the fifteenth day of the ninth month. Most days, there is a Cheshire Cat grin knowing that others are obliged to report to work by nine or earlier. Uninspired, it is tempting to delay writing until later in the day in anticipation that I may be more motivated to embrace my identity as a writer.

I need to resist reviewing my e-mails or returning phone calls. A real estate agent needs to start the day with phone calls. As a writer, the world needs to wait for a few hours. At some point, flexibility rather than discipline may be appropriate – not yet.

The challenge is to write. That's what writer's do. Uninspiring writing is still writing. Of course, it feels better when the turn of phrase I choose is precise and comes without effort, when the story line is coherent, and when I feel like a runner who has hit her stride. To expect that would happen every day would be to tempt failure.

Despite my extensive list of possible projects, I have managed to avoid being compulsive. To have several projects, concurrently in progress, works for me. Sometimes, I putter at one and move on to another. When the energy for one slips away, I find new energy again in yet another. Often a creative piece is followed by a piece that is demanding in a different way. To write about human experience is different than to prepare a reference list. I need to remember that both are writing.

Warming up

In the world of fitness there is a hard and fast guideline. Warm up before you start serious exercise. This morning, my writing muscle was sluggish, unresponsive to my expectation that it should immediately produce original and inspiring material. Diversion didn't work. Downloading my photo card was something that needed doing but didn't stimulate any new thought. Filling the dishwasher and running it was inevitable but the background hum didn't generate any verbal images. Soaking in the pain of the world as reported by BBC didn't prompt me to apply myself to any given writing project I have underway. Had we been at home, I am sure I could have conjured up numerous additional distractions.

Molly might have needed grooming, and although I would not allow myself a full-fledged digression into administrative tasks, I might have stopped and paid a few bills. However, at this moment, the flatness has stayed flat. So I am at a choice point. Admit resistance beyond recovery, bestow upon myself a reprieve, and simply accept there is a rhythm to my writing energy. Or try a warm up. Get on the writer's treadmill, the keyboard, and see if the writer warms up.

The coach in me wants to push her, pump up the adrenalin, and urge her with stern words. The dedicated professional self would have her sluggishly persist; averse to admitting lackluster for her cause. The challenge of living this new life is to remember I am a writer, not an athlete, not a resolute leader. This is more a matter of negotiation than enforcement. Just experiment. No pressure. No coercion. No imposing of sheer will. Instead engage in an unrelated topic, typing one word after another, one phrase after another as if taking one step after another. Just notice what happens.

Retain permission to stop if the activity intended to encourage is not beneficial. Stretch a little; behave as if I am in a stride, readying the author within to awaken from the slumber of apathy. Refuse to be concerned about how the lethargy crept in and forego anticipating that the imaginative capacities will be reluctant on any consistent basis. Just warm up.

Soaking up the silence

Spring on the acreage can be demanding. This year, the challenge is unexpectedly taxing. There are only my two hands, not the usual four. Fate has relegated Allen to gardening coach and occasional commander of the garden hose. He stands by for the inevitable moments when I stall the lawnmower and tangle the power hedge clippers. I argue with dandelion roots and confront dead rose branches on my quest for the beauty that inevitably arises from our efforts. There is a temptation to be at war with the earth, reshaping it according to my will. My body though acts as a mentor of patience. Two hours of raking and weeding, and seeding and weeding, and raking and seeding is all I can tolerate. The few times I have exceeded logical limits. The following day, my back bends and holds its form, like the plastic straws designed for the bedridden.

There is something rewarding in doing yard work. When the carrot tops peek through the earth, when the flowers blossom, when the beans sprout, it all seems worth while. When I walk the cleared paths, the sense that life is good or strong in a way that is different than walking in a city park.

Today it has been raining. The slow kind. The kind that soaks in. The kind that patters on the balcony. The kind that makes geraniums look more red. The kind that makes even the dog want to stay indoors.

There is still the chill of spring in the air. It was a muffin-making day, and there was time for tea. Tea with leaves, not bags. There was time for solitude and time for being with each other in silence. We both love those days.

It was easy to choose to write today. The decision to write, for the most part, was decreed by the weather. It was as if the rain said, "I will tend the gardens. You write. That quiet place awaits you. You haven't been there often these days. This time is yours to take." It is not whether to write. It is weather to write.

And I did. For nearly seven consecutive hours, I soaked up the silence, pen in hand, like the seedlings that I planted days ago are soaking up this gentle downpour.

Cycling with the seasons

The silence of the first snowfall has begun. It is time for the picnic table to be retired, for the car to take its place in the garage each day and time to fill the bird feeders more systematically. The kayaks are already sleeping in their racks, and the remnants of the garden were taken in last week. Winter seems so natural when I am relieved of the concerns of more treacherous driving, more layers of clothing, more day to day living delays.

Here there are no hurricanes, no earthquakes. However, a full fledged blizzard is potentially a serious threat, and even more so to the naïve who believe that proximity to civilization is a rationale for not wearing proper footwear.

In the past I hated every flake that fell and interrupted my life. In the last few years, I have noticed that the seasons are more natural than my reactions to them. Perhaps, so it is with life. If I can welcome the transitions, I too will change.

Is living the life of a writer simply a season? Am I entering the winter of my life when I feel it is only the autumn of my existence? In reality, winter is but one cycle, and I need to notice that the cycles of the seasons repeat endlessly, and the tulip bulbs will bloom in the spring. Winter is also the forerunner to beauty. Perhaps, like the animals that hibernate, I will have saturated my capacity for isolation and will be restless and hungry for something new and different.

Even in the years of intense career and family demands, I wrote between pressures. Often late into the night, but this was not the life of a writer. It was a life with some writing.

This winter feels different, not as if I am going to my cave to survive the elements, but rather as having the privilege to draw my reserves into focus. Not to be drained but to be replenished, perhaps to emerge, having given birth to that which is awaiting. Regardless, I am naming these *my writing years.*

Digging out of the drifts

A snowstorm is a writer's gift. There are no fierce howling winds today. More like the earth is sneezing and breathing. Sneezing and breathing. The snow on the spruce bows bends them toward the earth. Laden so heavily, the winds that differentiate a snowfall from a snowstorm choreograph the trees in a waltz performed by the whole forest. There's a hypnotic quality to snow – white on white, moving. In the more open spaces, it sifts across the landscape making art with texture and form, writing beauty into an otherwise bleak scene.

I welcome the retreat from the usual structures, from the errands that take me out of my writing space. I welcome the isolation that decades ago was so prolonged it drove prairie women to despair. Today's winter storm brings no hardship, no dread that the firewood will be depleted or that loved ones will freeze doing what is necessary despite the elements.

In the winter, as children we played store in the farm kitchen, drew pictures and helped mom bake cookies. We made hot chocolate from cocoa and real cream and loved having the dog inside. The hired man played checkers with us. We learned about sundogs and watched out the window while the Clydesdale team that Dad was so proud of pulled a stoneboat of feed to the cattle. We asked where the kittens were, and mom promised that they were safe and warm in the barn. We knew better than to ask to go outside.

A snowstorm still holds that mystery. Still demands the respect learned as a child. There is a natural pull to start the fire, steep a pot of tea, and write longhand before the flames. The lane, narrowed by multiple attempts to keep it open, will discourage visitors for a few days. Although it's not true, I enjoy imagining satellite reception has been interrupted. There will be silence and homemade soup for two days. Even the dog quietly accepts nature's interjection of solitude, curls up beside me, and waits for the inevitable pat that happens during creative pauses.

Finding the courage to hear

No one likes to write about being held hostage to illness, as a patient or as a caregiver. Books that whine don't sell. Writing about triumphing against all odds, about coping in the face of challenge, or about hoping in the midst of despair is far more acceptable.

I wonder how many private journals are hidden away that would testify that illness sucks. Illness sucks away the good energy. Illness steals motivation, and illness banishes creativity. Illness closes doors and narrows pathways.

The demands of illness rip at the soul of a writer tearing it from normalcy. In the end it renders either a wrenching exposé of reality or an apathy that parlyzes the pen.

No wonder professional writing sanitizes illness. One has "side effects" to chemotherapy. No one talks about puking into your soup bowl.

Schizophrenia is a "dis-order", like an incorrectly filled invoice. We don't want to hear about the confusion, the abandonment, or the shame. Language insulates us. Labels make the pain someone else's pain. A few depictions of the dark journeys reach publication, usually because they have some character building value. If we cannot bear to hear each other's pain, how can we write about it?

I don't want to hear about the 96 year old who was extracted from her community hospital because policy dictated that she accept the next available long term care bed. I don't want to hear how she pleaded. I don't want to know about the aloneness that swept over her as she was raised into the handi-bus for transfer. I don't want to ask her what it really felt like. If I do hear, I too will hurt. If I hurt though, perhaps then, I will tell her story.

Policy is written in lifeless words. Words that carry no feeling. Words that standardize practice. Words from the language of quality assurance. Imagine the difference if policy had to begin with three human stories and had include three inspiring words.

First though, we must have the courage to hear. The courage to hear that illness sucks, and poverty hurts, and loneliness harms.

If I have the courage to hear, then I will have the courage to write, the courage to use words to change the world.

My dad, Morris, at 90

Writing about the pain

Some things are painful to write about. If I write about them, I hurt. If I don't write about them, the hurt festers inside of me.

During the last chapter of dad's life I sat with him for many hours in his hospital room.

I am now grateful that these written words helped cleanse my wounds.

Signed and Sealed

Sitting beside the catheter
    reeking of concentrated urine
Crafting the thickened mucus
    in his raw mouth and throat
    onto soft pink sponges and
    learning to call it 'mouth care"
Witnessing the droop of his eye
    knowing it bothers him,
    a once handsome man
Attending the wound left by
    the violent retrieval of the tumor
    that haunted us all for weeks
Advocating and protecting him
    in a system overextended,
    long since corrupted
    by substituting
    technology for compassion.
Admiring this man
    grateful and dignified
    in these dark moments
Whispering encouragements
    in the morning twilight
    of his 90th birthday
Knowing that the pathology report
    has sealed his death.

Avoiding ambivalence

Every once in a while I have a piece that just doesn't work. I think I know what I want to say, and yet, the words just never convey the message. It is like a pumpkin dessert recipe I have never mastered. It is delicious when my sister-in-law Dawn makes it. For reasons unknown to me, even on my third attempt, I only approximated her results. The wrong size pan. Forgot the second egg. It didn't work with soymilk. I know it can be scrumptious but I just can't get it right. In my head, it's right there. On the paper, it just isn't working.

For example, I tried a piece about James Pennebaker's work. He is the researcher who has proven the mental and physical health benefits of writing. I spoke briefly with him at a conference in the Southern States years ago before he was well known. He sat in solitude at the end of a short hallway inhaling a cigarette like only those who know the tether of addiction. I wanted the piece I was writing to say two things: something about legitimizing writing for therapeutic purposes and something about the value of scholars writing in the vernacular for the general public.

I managed to discuss the legitimacy of raging and grieving and celebrating on paper, usually longhand in my journal in the quiet of my bedtime ritual. It is no longer just a ritual to get something off my chest. It is to get something out of my soul. To get the sputum out of my soul.

Helplessness, anger, and ill will are the pneumonia of the soul. Silent and deadly. They slowly choke off life. There has to be some place to vent the frustrations with the family's sense of entitlement, to fume at the shortsightedness of public policy, to meet the fears of tomorrow, and to wrestle with the regrets of yesterday.

When I tell men about the health benefits of writing, they write. Before the Pennebakers of the world, they looked at me with blank faces as if I was asking them to vomit at a dinner party.

The second point about scholars writing in the vernacular for the general public just never came together no matter how I muddled with it. Sometimes a piece just doesn't work.

It is okay for a piece not to work. Just let it go, not every piece will work!

Getting in the groove

The first writing retreat I took was at the Sylvia Hotel on English Bay near Stanley Park in Vancouver. I had notes and satchels of interviews and pads of paper. I was going to do a draft of the what would later become *It All Begins with Hope*. I rose at 7:00 a.m., worked until 9:00 a.m., had porridge in the restaurant, worked until 11:30, walked in Stanley Park with fruit and a granola bar, worked until 3:00 p.m., allowed myself an hour of television, worked until 6:00 p.m., ate at the Szechwan restaurant at the end of the street. The crisp broccoli that seemed to be in every dish was my daily staple. I chose to eat every supper there. Despite loving Indian cuisine and thinking about a feed of local fish, routine was part of the plan. Back to the computer at 7:30, I worked again until 9:00 p.m. Over and over for eight days. No change in venue. Was that compulsive or was it disciplined motivation?

I chose not to call anyone. Not to shop. Not to eat junk food.

As the days passed the intellectual lethargy of the first couple of days transformed into a capacity to see the bigger picture. I wasn't writing sentence by sentence or paragraph by paragraph. The stories were telling me how they needed to be assembled. I was experiencing my first writer's high. Writing was giving energy, not taking it.

If an eight day silent writing retreat garnished with Szechwan cuisine is a high, an extended drought of ideas and motivation is a low. I have witnessed the pain that the pressure to write can impose. I have seen students and colleagues hover over the keyboard for indefinite pauses.

No topic is so commonly addressed as writer's block, that seemingly unexplainable cessation of the attendance by the muse. There are as many recommended interventions as there are writers. In contrast, I rarely re-read a paragraph or a chapter while on a writer's high, that elated feeling of simply being on a roll and going with it. Writing doesn't have to be an effort, or a painful tugging.

Sometimes writing just flows. Sometimes I can get a high just writing.

Walking the Write Path

If you're not excited about it, it's not the right path to take.

Abraham Hicks

I am walking my own path, your approval is not actually required.

Ronna Fay Jevne

Wisdom is knowing the right path to take. Integrity is taking it.

Unknown

Wanting things easier

I want writing to be easier. I want the words to come quickly, the descriptions to be exact the first time. I want my thoughts to convey my intent without revision. I want to know my thoughts before I have given any thought to what I want to say. I want the printer to always work perfectly and the computer to never have glitches. I want to create cookbooks in my mind while I cut celery and to invent childrens' classics as I am telling stories to the grandchildren.

In other words, I am spoiled. I do not want to work hard at this. I don't want to put in hours to produce a paragraph or even a page. I want poetic phrases and intriguing metaphors that work to ooze out of me from some untapped cavern of talent. I want the advice about warming up to be for those other writers, not me. I want someone else to do the revisions. I want a ghostwriter to finish things when my passion wanes.

I don't want to do footnotes or write for permissions to use quotes. I want to be paid as much for speaking in public about writing as I was for speaking about death and dying. I want an agent to effortlessly discover me and to surprise me with a movie rights offer. While I am at it, I would like to be invited to be the writer-in-residence somewhere, actually anywhere would do. That way I could get out of the office and eat small sandwiches and be appreciated. And I could call my office a writing studio. And I want people to stop asking me how I am enjoying retirement.

Not being employed is different than being retired. I write. And I see clients. That makes me a writer and a therapist. The latter supports the privilege of being the writer. Both are versions of authoring. I am not retired!!

After I have one of these little tantrums I remind myself that it is my choice to be a writer. No one bribed me. I take my cup of hot lemon, pat Molly on the head, and go back to the keyboard. That's what writers do.

Or they call a friend and plead insanity.

Channeling energy for my writing

A waterfall generates energy by the sheer force of a body of water flowing into the depths below.

In the realm of writing, I sometimes experience a sense of flow. The ideas and the words come without a struggle.

Mihaly Csikszentmihalyi, in his book *Flow: The psychology of happiness,* defines flow as a state in which a person is so absorbed in a creative activity that nothing else seems important. In that state, the person enjoys a genuine satisfaction.

For me, there is an undefined relationship between the thieves of flow and the flow. I can't fully explain how they are connected. I know that when I am weary, the flow that I am talking about doesn't happen. I know when I am hurried, the flow doesn't happen. I know when I wordsmith, the flow doesn't happen.

In the 1970's there was an expresion, "Don't push the river, it flows by itself." My reputation as a go-getter, in my earlier professional life, isn't my greatest strength as a writer. It interferes with flow.

What else interferes with flow? I don't do well working with colleagues who micro-manage. It takes a lot of extra energy to stay pleasantly focused and yet not be diverted by their constant need for control.

Large and long social events of shallow conversation zonk me out. On the other hand, evenings with a small group, that offer more in-depth exchanges, energize me.

Long walks, quiet talks, forty laps in the pool, a nourishing meal eaten slowly, and times of sheer solitude replenish my energy. My reserve energy builds and flow returns on its' own.

As I approach my three score and ten years, there is a noticeable shift in my energy. It is quieter. To-do lists mean less. Minimizing the mundane means channeling more energy to creative activities, which in turn increases flow. I have come to terms with the facts that:

> I don't do hurry well anymore,
> I want my soul to stroll,
> I leave human racing to others.

I have writing to do.

Hitting a hole in one

I am not a golfer. I am at best a duffer. Being naturally athletic, at least I don't embarrass myself on those rare occasions when I don my sun visor, resurrect my 1977 clubs, and join friends who know fairway etiquette. Golfing has always been a bit slow for me while demanding on a reluctant bursitic hip. I have rarely used a cart. Golfing is a bit hard on the ego as well. Like so many things in life, it requires skill, and it takes practice.

I did though once hit a hole in one. It seemed perfectly natural. It was a short hole. With a six iron, I took what felt like a natural swing and in it went. At that time, I didn't know how rare it is to hit a hole in one. Golfing would be a painful activity if I expected a hole in one, even on occasion; a hole in one in the writing business is rare.

In *Bird By Bird*, Anne Lamott in her essay "Shitty First Drafts" informs us that almost all good writing begins with terrible first efforts. On rare occasion, I have written a first draft that pleased me. Not often though.

In the early 1990s, I hid away in a cabin on the beautiful shore of the sunshine coast. I wrote a 175 page draft of a book entitled *Interdisciplinary Perspectives on Hope*. I still have those pages. Writing those pages turned out to be what I needed to do in order to write what my heart really wanted to write, what I needed to write. That wasn't a hole in one. It was three full golf courses just to get to a putting green!!

It takes time and pages to get the extraneous sorted out from the essence in my head. I often need to write page after page before head and heart are ready for the partnership.

Sometimes writing is like a novice playing golf. A beautiful drive down the center. An Arnold Palmer paragraph. Sometimes the fairways get written with ease, and I can't sink the putt. That final phrase that completes the paragraph evades me. It takes me many strokes to finish the round.

Taking the time

It all takes time. I don't deny that there are those moments when the creativity flows onto the page and never needs to be revisited. They are rare though. Even when I think I have been brilliant, usually late at night, I am not nearly as impressed the next morning. Writing often needs seasoning.

It takes time to find the focus that is truly the arrow that I want to send into flight. It takes time to do background reading. It takes time to craft a first sentence. It takes time to do that "shitty first draft" that Anne Lamott speaks of in *Bird by Bird*. It takes time and patience to let the ideas emerge and to find the sequence that flows. It takes time to vary the sentence lengths. It takes time to create parallel structure. It takes time to eliminate the redundancies. It takes time to see where what I just wrote fits in a larger manuscript. It takes time to remember when to use a comma and when to use a semi-colon, even though I have been doing this for years. It would help if manuals quit changing the rules. It all takes time.

It takes time to rework the working title. It takes time to do the footnotes. I recently discovered we no longer use "Ibid" and "Op Cit" in referencing. It takes time to check the references and to find the reference for that quote I love, the source of which I forgot to write down. It takes time to get feedback. It takes time to select and contact sources of potential blurbs and more time to wait for their responses. It takes time, if one goes with a commercial publisher, to write book proposals and send query letters. It takes time to learn about social media marketing and on-demand printing.

I feel like I can detect a book that has been dictated. I can't know of course, but I can suspect. Somehow the flow is different. Somehow the first chapters are strong and the remaining chapters fade. If the author hasn't taken the time, something is missing. Something perhaps intangible but necessary. I am always comforted when I hear or read that an author has taken months, if not years, to produce a particular manuscript.

Envisioning the gift

Deena Metzger in *Writing for Your Life*, encourages us to see writing as "a sacred act of conscience because the writer has been given the gift of stories, insight, vision, images and words, on behalf of the community. What we say, how we say it, to whom we speak, these are urgent considerations. As an old-fashioned writer, I believe in literature and the power of the word. I believe that writing is inspired by and serves intelligence and beauty". She reminds us that "writing is an ethical act and that the writer has responsibilities to herself, to community, and to spirit; and so must be diligent and devoted in her search for meaning and truthfulness."

That quote is taped to my ink blotter. It reminds me that, without writers, much of the beauty and intelligence available in the world would not be shared; much of the world's injustice would remain invisible. Reading *Our Endangered Values* by Jimmy Carter made me think. It made me want to be part of the solution, not part of the problem. Reading *Hope in the Darkness* by Rebecca Solnit made me believe that I can be part of making the world a better place, that it takes all of us doing whatever it is that we do.

In junior high school, I was interested in writing. I knew how to get good grades out of Miss Blanch. Simply write flowery fluff. She loved it. I loved the good grades and learned nothing about writing. In high school, I took a creative writing course from an eccentric who let us write on colored paper. I did not perceive myself as gifted. Indeed, I wasn't. The seeds were there though in the piece I wrote about nuclear arms for the school paper. It would take years to develop a sense of depth, a sense that what I felt at the bedside of a dying teenager, or kayaking in the Sea of Cortez in a storm had any value beyond myself. It would take years to recognize a gift was emerging.

I now acknowledge the gift to me, my desire to strengthen the gift, and my joy of humbly sharing the gift. I want the stories, insight, vision, images, and words that I write to be motivated by my yearning for a better community, a better earth, a kinder world.

Writing moves my soul

It is increasingly obvious to me that I not only want to live my life as a writer; I want to live my life as a certain kind of writer. A continual refining process is occurring, subtly defining the parameters of the writing to which I am drawn. Precisely what that is has neither revealed itself sufficiently to name it as a genre, nor been convincing as the signature of my work.

Words like "reflective" or "contemplative" are in the ballpark, but they feel unattached to the energy I feel when I write. Forcing a name to my style may be drawing premature boundaries. Maybe writing what moves me is all I need to attend to at this time. What would we call that? There is no "whatever moves me" genre. I suppose, ultimately, that is what every author writes.

I wonder if musicians have this sense of being called to a genre. Do they innately know if they are classical violinists or fiddlers? How far will they stray from their intuitive home?

Knowing what I don't want to write is easier. Sometimes when I launch a piece and it doesn't flow, it is like a tennis player who stepped over the service line. Something feels violated. Other times, it is like the fate of someone who is orienteering, and having missed the marker, is well along the wrong path before the error is detected. Some sixth sense calls her to a halt. Only through awareness can she recover. She must trust that something isn't right.

So it is with an occasional choice I make. I am still learning that because I am able to write something doesn't mean it is what I am called to write. A conference presentation may still be an expression of my values, be a contribution to the community, and an assurance that I remain a capable thinker. It takes me to an older life, a life I have left. Return visits to that life are fine. I just need to remind myself not to overstay my visit. Just like agreeing to complete a labour intensive writing project for a community event, it is a reminder to avoid the seduction of being needed.

Diversions are teachable moments. The sooner that I recognize a diversion, the sooner that I return to writing that moves my soul.

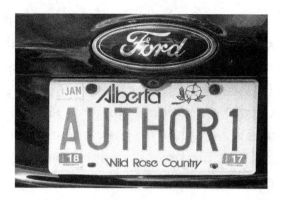

Going public

A personalized license plate seems to me to be the ultimate in self-indulgence. Surely the funds could better be used to support a child overseas, or supply blankets to earthquake victims, or bolster the local food bank that, despite us living in the wealthiest province in our country, seems to have burgeoning needs. There is no defense within my value system for having a license plate for the sheer hell of it. I do though love my license plate. It was my birthday present.

WRITER1 was gone. That is, someone already had that plate identification. I got *AUTHOR1* which leaves little to misunderstand and, on occasion, generates conversation. The young oil lube technician servicing our car inquired:

"Which one of you is a writer?"

   reply: "We both are".
"No kidding?""What do you write?"
Without pause, he continued:

"That is so neat. I have always wanted
to write. I love it. I haven't written much since I left
high school. I love to write science fiction kind of stuff.
There isn't much time to do it right
now. But I would love to be a writer."

   reply: "Don't give up the dream."
"I haven't but you are the first people that I have met
who are real writers."

   *reply: "Did you know there is a writer's group
here?*
"No kidding."

   reply: "No kidding."
"That would be neat. Can anyone join?"

   *reply: "Anyone can join. They meet on the first
Wednesday of every month."*

   As we drove away, it seemed that every penny we
had paid for the personalized plate was well spent. If
one young writer is moved, in even a tiny way, closer
to being part of the writing community, closer to his
dream, I don't resent a cent. There was a moment of
pride. A moment when living life as a writer seemed
important to more than me. How many of us are out
there, changing oil, working in bakeries, doing day
jobs waiting for the writer to have a place in our lives?

Becoming a pilgrim

Perhaps in each of us who makes an intentional choice to live our life as a writer, there is a pilgrim. Someone who feels the longing, hears the call, and departs knowing the way will be difficult at times.

It is often a lonely path, sometimes a stormy one, sometimes an uncertain one, but it is the path we walk. The path we choose. The path that perhaps has chosen us. We are not the dabbler. Not the once in a lifetime historian of our journey. Not the journaler who turns to the page only in times of distress. Not the conference or workshop junkie who is in search of who to emulate and who loves to talk about whose workshop they most recently attended. We may or may not be a teacher of writing. Some teachers of writing live their lives as teachers, some of necessity, some by choice.

I am a pilgrim with a pen. Who will journey with me? Who will I meet on the path? Who will offer a hand and who will resent my presence? Where will I find shelter? How will I open myself to that which is uncomfortable or even repulsive to see? How will I deal with the ache of what I cannot alter? What images will become indelible? Which images will fade almost without notice? How often will I laugh and what will bring a tear to my eye? Who will be my greatest mentors?

As I embark on this pilgrimage, which I expect to be at least a decade, I understand that there may be few who understand my pace. A friend recently disclosed she did the famous Camino pilgrimage and how arduous she found the experience, at times, many times, having to call upon her anger to complete the day's objective. For me, the pilgrimage will not be about grueling schedules and public profile. I long for something very different in this decade. Something I cannot yet name, yet something I sense is well on its way. Something quiet without removing adventure; something deliberate yet without the loss of spontaneity. Something that will craft a deeper side of me. Something that will open the next door.

Armstrong, K. 1994. *The History of God: The 4,000 - Year Quest of Judaism, Christianity and Islam.* New York: Ballentine Books.

Bender, S. 2001. *Keeping a Journal You Love.* Cincinnati, Ohio: Walking Stick Press.

Berger, J. 1997. *Photocopies.* New York: Vintage Books.

Brown, D. 2009. *Da Vinci Code.* New York: Anchor Books.

Boyko, J. 2006. *Into the Hurricane: Attacking Socialism and the CCF.* Winnipeg, Manitoba: J. Gordon Shillingford Publishing Inc.

Callwood, J. in Sheilds, C. & Anderson, M. (editors). 2000. *Dropped Threads: What We Aren't Told.* Toronto, Ontario: Vintage Canada.

Cameron, J. 1999. *The Right to Write.* New York: Putman, Inc.

Canin, E. 2001. *Carry Me Across the Water.* New York: Random House.

Carter, J. 2006. *Our Endangered Values: Americas Moral Crisis.* New York: Simon and Shuster Paperbacks.

Coelho, P. 1999. *Veronica Decides to Die.* Hammersmith, London: Harper Collins Publishers.

Costanzo, C. 1999. *The Twelve Gifts of Birth.* New York: Harper Resource.

Csikszentmihalyi, M., (1990). *Flow: The Psychology of Optimal Experience.* New York: Harper Collins Publishers

Dillard, A. 1989. *The Writing Life.* New York: Harper and Row Publishers.

Douglas, L. 1946. *Doctor Hudson's Secret Journal.* Toronto, Ontario: Thomas Allen, Limited.

Graff, J., Wann, D., & Naylor, T. 2001. *Affluenza.* San Francisco, CA: Berrett-Koehler Publishers Inc.

Grumback, D. 1994. *Fifty Years of Solitude.* Boston: Beacon Press.

Flaherty, A. 2005. *The Midnight Disease.* New York: Marine Books.

Hart, P. (Ed.) 2002. *Survival or Prophecy: The Letters of Thomas Merton and Jean Lecerq.* New York: Farrar Straus & Giroux.

Jevne, R. 1991. *It All Begins With Hope.* San Diego, California: LuraMedia.

Johnson, S. 1999. *Sea Kayaking: A Woman's Guide.* Camden Maine: Ragged Mountain Press.

King, S. 2000. *On Writing: A Memoir of The Craft.* New York: Scribner.

Krementz, J. 1996. *The Writer's Desk.* New York: Random House.

Langer, E. 2005. *On Becoming an Artist: Reinventing Yourself Through Mindful Creativity.* New York: Ballentine Books.

LeClare, A. 2009. *Listening Below the Noise.* New York: Harper Collins

Lamott, A. 1994. *Bird by Bird: Some Instructions on Writing and Life.* New York: Anchor Books.

Lindberg, A. 1955, 1975. *The Gift of the Sea.* New York: Pantheon Books.

Lutz, G. & Stevenson, D. 2005. *The Writer's Digest Grammar Desk Reference.* Cincinnati, Ohio: Writers Digest Books.

Marai, S. 2002. *Embers.* New York:Vintage Books.

Metzger, D. 1992. *Writing for Your Life: A Guide and Companion to Inner Worlds.* New York: Harper Collins Publishers.

Nelson, L. 2004. *Writing and Being.* Makawao, Maui, Hawaii: Inner Ocean Publishing.

Progoff, I. 1992. *At a Journal Workshop.* New York: Dialogue House.

Rowling, J.K. 1997. *Harry Potter Series* London: Bloomsbury Press.

Runback, D. 1994. *Fifty Days of Solitude.* Boston, Massachusetts: Beacon Press.

Sarton, M. 1984. *At Seventy.* New York: W.W. Norton.

Solnit, R. 2004. *Hope in the Dark: Untold histories with possibilities.* Toronto: Penguin Group.

Sorin, F. 2004. *Digging Deep.* New York: Time Warner Book Group.

Sternberg, R. 1990. *Wisdom: Its nature origins and development.* New York: Cambridge University Press.

Thompson, J. 2000. *Making Journals by Hand.* Gloucester, Massachusetts: Rockport Publishers Inc.

Ueland, B. 1938. *If You Want to Write.* St. Paul, Minnesota: Graywolf Press.

Ugresic, D. 2003. *Thank You for Not Reading.* Translation by Celia Hawkesworth. Dalkey Archive Press.

Wagamese, R. 2003. *For Joshua.* Anchor Canada.

PHOTO CREDITS

About the Author

Ronna Fay Jevne

Ronna Jevne is a professor emeritus of the University of Alberta. Her career has spanned decades as a teacher, psychologist, professor, inspirational speaker, and the author of more than a dozen books.

She shares her love of writing, particularly reflective writing with students, patients, health care professionals, high needs adolescents, inmates, correctional officers, and many others who enjoy the benefits of writing to enhance well-being.

Ronna lives in a quiet rural setting with her husband Hal who shares the love of writing.

Ronna and Hal share their commitment to writing through the Prairie Wind Writing Centre. *prairiewindwritingcentre.ca*

What is your Inner Author doing?

Join Ronna and Hal for an *Inner Author workshop* to explore your relationship with writing. Get to know *your inner author.*

Whether you write the occasional poem, pour your heart out onto the pages of a journal, or have a project underway or in mind, *Your Inner Author will invite you to explore* your relationship with the part of you that is drawn to writing.

In a safe and creative setting, using guided writing, discussion and readings to *get to know your inner author.* Explore your history, strengths, needs, frustrations and delights. Increase your sense of how to support and *encourage your inner author.*

The act of writing is a complex experience. It is not just developing a structure and choosing the words. Writing is often an experience that interacts with our personal values and feelings. With rare exception, the writing process involves a dance between the writer and the writing. The unique aspect of the seminar is that we will use writing to explore our beliefs, feelings and behaviours related to writing.

Visit our web site: prairiewindwritingcentre.ca